Contents

Section One : **Current Status and Concerns**

1 Funding Public School Systems: A 25 Year Review 9
   François Gendron
2 The Impact Of Changes In Federal Provincial Block Transfers . . 25
   Dan Perrins
3 School Reforms And Financial Considerations: A Policy Analysis 35
   Y.L. Jack Lam
4 The Decentralization Of Public School Systems:
   Some Financial Implications 47
   Anne L. Jefferson
5 Financing Aboriginal Education 55
   K.P. Binda

Section Two : **Possible Solutions and Prospects**

6 Towards A Better Understanding of Economic Contribution
   of the Public School 77
   Y.L. Jack Lam
7 Promoting Equity, Adaptability and Efficiency in Public
   School Systems Through Alternative Resource Allocation 89
   Stephen B. Lawton
8 Eking Out the Last Dollars: Nontraditional Funding
   for Education 105
   Vivian Hajnal and Keith Walker
9 Chaperonic Reflections On the Relations Between Business
   and Education Sectors 113
   Keith Walker and Brent Kay
10 Program Delivery: What New Technology Promises 129
   Arnold Novak
11 Leading With Less: Leadership Issues in a Time of
   Financial Constraint 139
   Patrick J. Renihan and Frederick I. Renihan

The Authors

François Gendron, Senior Analyst, Statistics Canada

Dan Perrins, Assistant Deputy Minister, Department of Education, Saskatchewan

Y.L. Jack Lam, Professor and Chair, Graduate Studies, Faculty Education, Brandon University, Manitoba

Anne L. Jefferson, Professor, Department of Educational Administration, Faculty of Education, University of Ontario

K.P. Binda, Associate Professor, Brandon University Northern Teacher Education Program, Manitoba

Stephen B. Lawton, Professor, Department of Educational Administration, Ontario Institute for Studies In Education/ University of Toronto, Ontario

Keith Walker, Associate Professor, Department of Educational Administration, College of Education, University of Saskatchewan

Vivian Hajnal, Associate Professor, Department of Educational Administration, College of Education, University of Saskatchewan

Brent Kay, Assistant Registrar, University of Saskatchewan

Arnold Novak, Associate Professor, Chair, Department of Administration, Faculty of Education, Brandon University

Patrick J. Renihan, Professor & Head, Department of Educational Administration, College of Education, University of Saskatchewan

Frederick I. Renihan, Superintendent of Schools, Surrey School Board, British Columbia

Education Finance

Current Canadian Issues

Y.L. Jack Lam

Editor

Detselig Enterprises Ltd.

Calgary, Alberta

© 1998 by Y.L. Jack Lam
Brandon University

Canadian Cataloguing in Publication Data
Main entry under title:
Education finance

Includes bibliographical references.
ISBN 1-55059-175-4
   1. Education – Canada – Finance.   I. Lam, Y.L. Jack.
   LB2826.6.C2E38   1988   379.1'1'0971   C98-910733-7

Detselig Enterprises Ltd.
210, 1220 Kensington Rd. NW
Calgary, Alberta T2N 3P5

Detselig Enterprises Ltd. appreciates the financial assistance from the Department of Canadian Heritage for its 1998 publishing program.

All rights reserved. No part of this book may be reproduced in any form or by any means without permission in writing from the publisher.

Printed in Canada   SAN 115-0324   ISBN 1-55059-175-4

Preface

Propelled by the desire to strike budget balances, and driven by the need to achieve greater fiscal accountability, both the federal government and the provincial governments across Canada have unleashed a series of measures that have radically altered the education landscape of the country in a matter of a few years. Indeed, one cannot comprehend any single major change in education without linking it to the financial motives of the governments.

A case in point is the radical transformation of governance structure in the education system. Notable among the devices that fall into this category is the passing of legislative acts in many provincial governments which steadily increase the power the ministers of education at the expense of the other pertinent stake holders. The propelling motive driving such a change reflects a profound distrust of educators in general and the school boards in particular, to put the financial situation in proper order. Likewise, the district/division consolidation in many provinces, the encouragement of resource sharing among neighboring jurisdictions in others, unveil a clear purpose of the provincial governments in saving substantial education dollars in response to the cutback of federal transfer. Even the creation of parent advisory councils, with varying degrees of power (i.e., replacement of school boards in New Brunswick and serving as the advisory bodies or watchdogs in other provinces) and in the name of greater grassroot input, is obviously another device for enhancing public control of its school system.

As the lion's share of the funding of public education goes to support the salary of school personnel, the current effort of cost cutting cannot be considered complete without looking into this dimension. The tempering of collective bargaining procedures, in unmistaken gesture of breaking the traditional power of teacher organizations, undoubtedly harbor the governments' intent of curtailing the escalating cost of annual increments demanded by the teaching professionals. The revisitation of teachers' compensation, as in the case of Manitoba, further confirms the government's intention of streamlining teachers' salary scales.

Given the persistent demands for regulating public funding within the acceptable fiscal confines, it becomes evident that even curriculum reorganization and the intensification of testing the learning outcomes (largely through the mandated provincial examinations at critical levels), carries the undebatable notion that public education should be efficiently operated to justify billions of dollars that are annually channelled into the education system. The once "domesticated enterprises," immune from the public scrutiny, as the education system had once been characterized, is no longer valid in the pervasive push for "higher productivity." The recent and not so recent emphasis of greater parental choice in schools and programs for their children further intensifies severe competition among schools and school divisions/districts, not dissimilar to those in the private enterprises.

While we might be at the tail end of the financial crises as the federal government and most provincial counterparts have balanced their books, it is doubtful that the governments will reverse the trend that they have set for the public school systems. For one thing, the national and provincial debts are still heavy and these continue to haunt the politicians and ensure them to be financially prudent. For another thing, the provincial governments, once have the fore-taste of success in trimming the funding of public education without too much political backlash, will find little incentive to return to the previous status quo. These imply that all the changes and features associated with restructuring are going to stay for some time to come.

The impetus for preparing this book comes from three different sources. First, I was struck by the lack of texts from the Canadian source in education finance. Year after year, in teaching graduate classes in this discipline, I have to borrow from the American sources to deal with the theoretical conceptualization and a few articles in journals to bring them up to date on some of the current issues. I approach my colleagues in other institutions to see how they cope with this issue. We end up all agreeing that this is too glaring a gap to be continually ignored. Hence, this collective undertaking is launched.

A second impetus comes from my experience as the Director of Canadian Education Association Leadership Short Course between the period of 1995 to 1997. In 1996, the theme that I chose was "School renewal in a period of Financial Constraints." In planning for the session, quite a few individuals in the Planning Committee mentioned that the financial issues could be too dry or too boring for many educators. Yet, it seemed evident that in dealing with almost all the crucial education changes these days, we could not overlook the financial motives, financial challenges and financial implications. The feedback of participants in this Short Course convinced me that while these senior administrators and education leaders were no expert in this domain, they were intrigued by agenda of the governments so preoccupied with their financial considerations in their recent initiatives.

A third impetus comes from the relative deficiency in the knowledge of finance among public educators. When the media sensationalizes the "waste" of public education, the "ineffectiveness" of the school operation and questions the "cost-benefit" of supporting the public schools, very few educators are ready to counter argue the extreme bias views. It would seem that unless that they are ready to take up the challenges, there will be no one to come to their defence.

This text is organized into two main sections with two interrelated themes that aim at enlightening us about the Canadian education finance. Section I furnishes a broad picture of the current status of education finance in Canada and the related concerns. One of the persistent concerns for the public is the on-going rising cost of funding public schools even though school enrolment is on the decline. Chapter 1 provides, therefore, an overview of the financing Canadian school systems over the past two and half decades, analyzing the causes for the rise of education expenditures.

As the battles for balancing the budget rages on, it is intriguing to know how the federal government manipulates with the federal-provincial transfers and what impacts these might have for funding public education at different levels. Chapter 2 takes on an "insider's look" at the whole situation.

Logically, the significant decrease of federal transfer exerts a domino effect on provincial governments and compounds their own problems of achieving balanced budgets. Chapter 3 documents, as an example, the struggle of Manitoba government to bring the financial chaos under control through a series of legislative acts. In brief, by passing these legislative acts, the managerial power of public education is further centralized in the hand of the provincial government, the autonomy of school divisions/districts is further curtailed, parental choices of schools and program are legitimized, allowing competitions among school jurisdictions to take shape, and clear guidelines in collective bargaining are imposed so that salary demands from teacher organizations will not get out of hand.

Ironically, at the local level, earlier attempts of school reforms when decentralization and diversification of the types of schools were the norms rather than exceptions, become entangled with the present cost-cutting efforts. Chapter 4 identifies the ambiguity and dilemmas of public educators in accommodating divergent needs of students while trying to operate under financial restraints. The description of the current concerns of education finance in Canada will not be completed without touching on the funding of aboriginal education. Chapter 5 documents in details the long struggle of the First Nations for gaining fiscal control in their quest for self-control and self-government.

The theme permeating Section II of this text zeros in on the search for some possible solutions and prospects regarding the current financial crunch. In the haste of redressing financial woes, political leaders at both federal and provincial levels tend to be somewhat disoriented in the sense that they treat public education in the same category as other public services. They slashed and chopped education budget as if education were another "money-eating" machine, rather than viewed it as a "human capital" investment. Chapter 6 therefore, provides a reorientation to such lost vision, reemphasizing the vital social and economic roles education plays in the individual, community, regional, social and national development.

A persistent challenge facing public school administrators in time of fiscal restraint is how do we preserve equity without sacrificing efficiency or vice versa. Chapter 7 outlines a thought-provoking proposal of achieving the seemingly irreconcilable purposes through alternative resource allocation.

Following the same trend of thought, it would seem only too selfevident to most school administrators, that traditional sources of funding public education are becoming less and less reliable. Rather than passively stretching the dwindling resources to meet program and personnel needs, Chapter 8 advocates that a more aggressive approach is needed for public education leaders to explore non-conventional sources of subsidizing the school operation.

In such a venture, the increasingly popular partnership forged between school and business to generate new resources for schools needs to be closely examined. Chapter 9 embarks on some serious reflection upon the advantages and disadvantages of fostering this kind of linkages. The emergent moral and ethical considerations and the tough choices that education leaders have to be made are explored.

Amidst the review of the full spectrum of reactive and proactive strategies in coping with the current financial restraint, one promising solution that lures in the horizon is the greater utilization of new technologies in program delivery. Chapter 10 focuses on the recent advances in technology and argues how technology enhances accessibility, accommodates diversity of learners' abilities, meets curriculum needs and achieves cost-effectiveness.

Confronted with growing public demands and diminished resources, leadership in the public education has been put to great test in terms of endurance and vitality. It seems logical therefore to conclude this book with Chapter 11 that looks at leadership issues in a time of financial constraint.

While the major emphasis of this text is education finance and should be used as a main reference for graduate students in this area, it is my hope that the text should lend itself readily to other education graduate courses that examine current concerns about governance, policy, program, school reforms, aboriginal education and leadership issues. The close inter-connectedness of political, economic, social and cultural changes in recent reform should be obvious and should provide fresh perspectives in examining some prevailing issues.

Y.L. Jack Lam

Section One

Current Status and Concerns

1
Funding Public School Systems: A 25-Year Review

François Gendron

Introduction

During the last few years, education in Canada has received tremendous attention not only from the traditional major stakeholders like governing authorities and teacher unions, but most noticeably from the business community, the media, and the general public.[1] The increased interest for education matters stems from a general concern with the quality of education and the amount of public resources allocated to it. At the same time, Canada is facing a period of severe budget constraints and governments are under pressure to eliminate annual deficits and reduce public debt which means less money available for publicly supported programs like education.

While the financing of education is being reviewed to cope with the current budget situation, there is a growing consensus that our overall competitiveness as a nation in the global market is closely linked to the quality of our education system. This link is crucial if Canadians are to maintain their standard of living in an increasing competitive market where technological innovation represents a constant challenge. But given the current context, is Canada investing enough in education? The purpose of this chapter is not to provide a definite answer to that question but rather to shed some light on the major trends affecting education costs and to compare Canada's investment in this sector with that of other OECD countries.[2]

The massive effort devoted to education in Canada during the last few decades has contributed to a gradual rise in the population's level of schooling. Today, Canada ranks among the top Organization for Economic Co-operation and Development (OECD) countries in terms of educational attainment. 81% of Canadians aged 25-34 had at least high school diploma in 1992, compared to 49% for the generation aged 55 to 64. The only other OECD nations who made more rapid progress are Finland and Sweden (Figure 1). Most noticeably,

Canada has the highest rate of postsecondary education (46%) compared with 31% in the United States. The overall figure for the OECD countries is 19%.

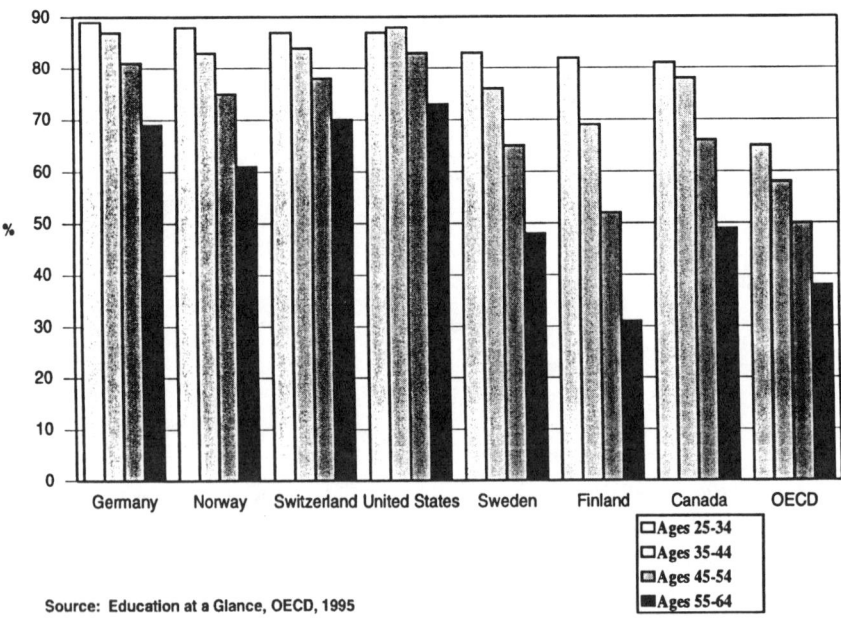

Source: Education at a Glance, OECD, 1995

Figure 1: Persons Having Attained at Least Upper Secondary Education, 1992

Canada would not be in such an enviable position if it had not invested a great deal of money in education. Like Finland and Sweden, Canada's investment on primary and secondary education amounts to approximately 4.6% of its gross domestic product (GDP); the OECD average is 3.7% (Figure 2).

Although spending on education as a proportion of GDP is widely used as an indicator for international comparisons, many education analysis and policy makers have difficulty interpreting its meaning and understanding the factors affecting it. In the following sections the factors behind spending on primary and secondary education in Canada will be analyzed. Trends in education expenditures[3] across Canada's four regions from 1970 to 1995 will also be presented. Expenditures will be examined relative to student enrolment and GDP per capita. Total salaries for educators,[4] which make up the bulk of primary and secondary education expenses, and the average number of students per educator will also be reviewed since they directly affect expenditures per student. Some other socio-demographic considerations influencing education expenditures will also be explored: for example, the age structure of the population and the participation rate of the school-age population.

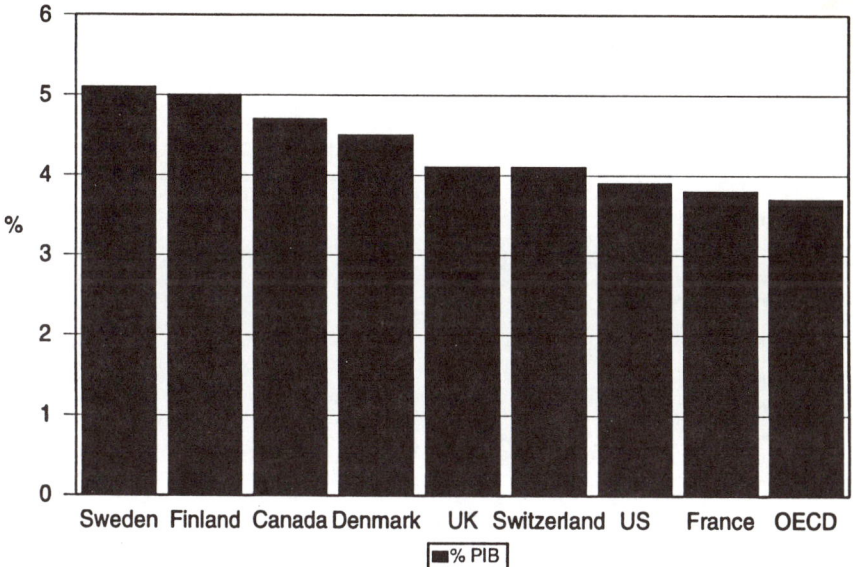

Source: Education at a Glance, OECD 1995 and STC

Figure 2: Public Educational Expenditure per GDP, Selected Countries, 1992

Overall Decline

Total spending on primary and secondary education as a proportion of GDP decreased from 5.5% in 1970 to 4.6% in 1995 (Figure 3). Although this may appear small relative to GDP, this 0.9 percentage point drop represents $7 billion annually in 1995-6 education dollars. The drop was particularly noticeable for Quebec, which saw its share of GDP fall from 6.4% in 1970 to 4.5% by 1995, a 1.9 percentage point decrease. As will be discussed later, major salary cuts in Quebec's public sector in 1982 played a major role in the province's sharp decline in education spending. The decreases in the Eastern provinces were also significant while the West and Ontario recorded slower and relatively more moderate decreases (-0.8 and -0.4 percentage points respectively).

How should one interpret these changes in spending per GDP? What causes regional variations? Breaking down or decomposing total spending as a proportion of GDP into three major factors – financing effort, demography, and participation – is one way to provide answers to these questions. The financing effort is defined as the amount of spending per student relative to GDP per capita; the demographic factor refers to the size of the school-age population relative to total population; and the participation factor is the proportion of school enrolment to the school-age population. The decomposition model used for this analysis (see Figure 4) relates these three factors to spending as a proportion of GDP.

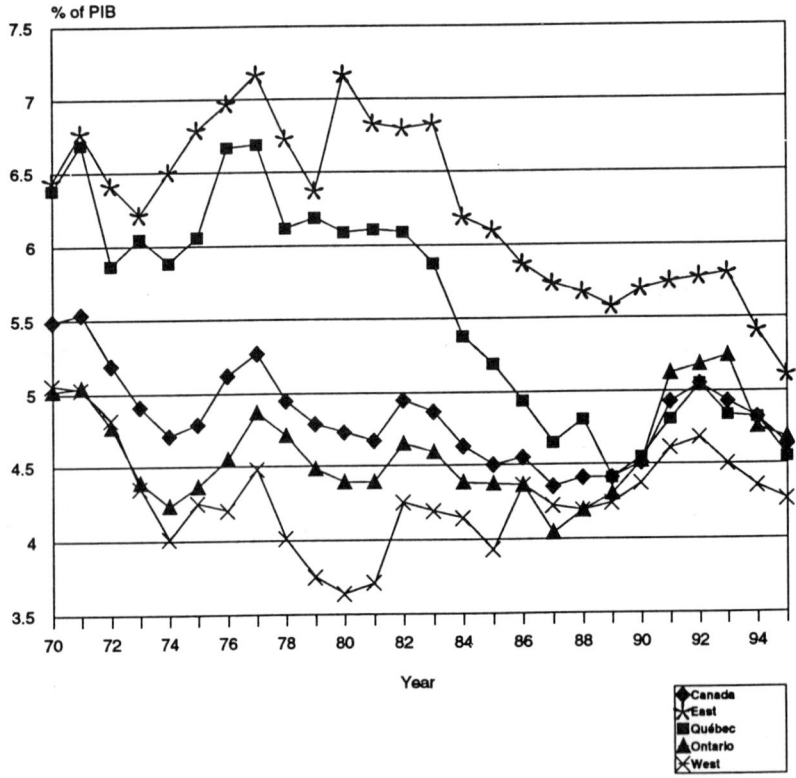

Figure 3: Educational Expenditure per GDP 1997 to 1995

To assess how a single factor contributes to the overall change in spending as a proportion of GDP, one can assume that all other factors are constant. For example, a higher participation rate or relatively younger population would imply more spending if the remaining variables (cost per pupil, GDP per capita, and so on) remain constant.

The Financing Effort

The financing effort for Canada as a whole increased from 21% in 1970 to 26% in 1995 (Figure 5). This percentage represents the average level of resources allocated to education for each student relative to the economy's capacity to pay as measured by GDP per capita. The overall increase in financing effort during the 25 year period under review can be explained by a sustained progression in spending per student (8.6% annually on average) which was not totally supported by the growth in the overall average wealth of the country (7.6%)

Total spending as a proportion of GDP is an aggregate measure of the amount spent in a specific sector relative to the overall economy. The following formula highlights the financing effort, demographic and participation factors affecting spending in the education sector:

Spending per GDP = Financing effort × Demographic × Participation

$$\frac{SPE}{GDP} = \frac{SPE}{STU} \times \frac{1}{GDP/POP} \times \frac{\text{5-19 age group}}{POP} \times \frac{STU}{\text{5-19 age group}}$$

SPE/GDP is the proportion of Gross Domestic Product spent on education.

SPE/STU is the average spending per student: a measure of the unit cost of educating a student.

GDP/POP is the Gross Domestic Product per capita: a measure of the relative wealth of a country and/or its capacity to pay.

5-19/POP is the proportion of school-age individuals in the population: a measure of the youthfulness of the population; when the 65 and over are included, this ratio is referred to as the dependency ratio.

STU/5-19 is the proportion of the school-age population actually enrolled in schools: a gross measure of participation.

Adapted from *Public Spending on Education*, OECD, Paris, 1986.

Figure 4: The Decomposition Model

The level of spending per student is directly affected by the dollars spent from school budgets on education "inputs" (educators and other staff salaries, school supplies, and so on) as well as by the number of pupils educated. In economic terms, one would refer to spending per student as the ratio of output to input, i.e. the productivity function of the sector.

During the 25-year period the price of education inputs did not rise disproportionately relative to other prices in the economy.[5] The Education Price Index, which measures price changes of a fixed basket of goods and services purchased by school boards, increased an average 6.4% annually since 1970 compared with 6.0% for the Consumer Price Index.

The increase in educators' salary rates, the main component of school operating expenditures (two thirds of school board operating expenditures) more or less followed general inflation during the period. This is not surprising since many teacher contracts contain provisions for indexing salary scales based on inflation. From 1970 to 1995, the salary rates of educators increased 6.3% on average, compared with 6% for the CPI, 6.4% for non-educator staff and 6.7% for non-salary items.

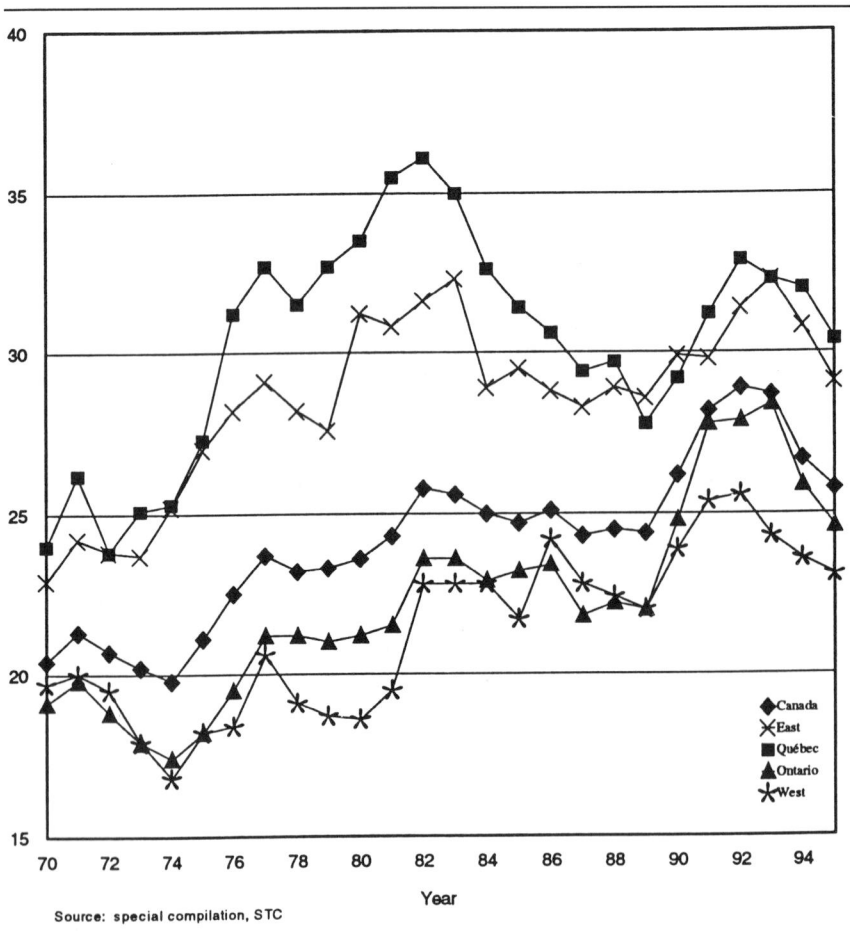

Figure 5: Financing Effort for Education 1970 to 1995

Although salary rates for educators did not grow much more than inflation (and even grew more slowly than other school budget inputs), the aging of the teaching force was such that many educators moved to higher salary categories as they gained more experience. This situation, combined with increases in salary scales, created an upward pressure on the overall average salary (calculated as the total educator salary bill divided by the total number of educators[6]) which went from $9 145 in 1970 to $59 050 in 1995 (Figure 6). This amounts to a 7.7% average annual increase, above inflation, but still not significantly above Canada's capacity to pay as measured by GDP per capita (which increased 7.6% annually on average). Thus other factors must have contributed to the noted increase in financing effort.

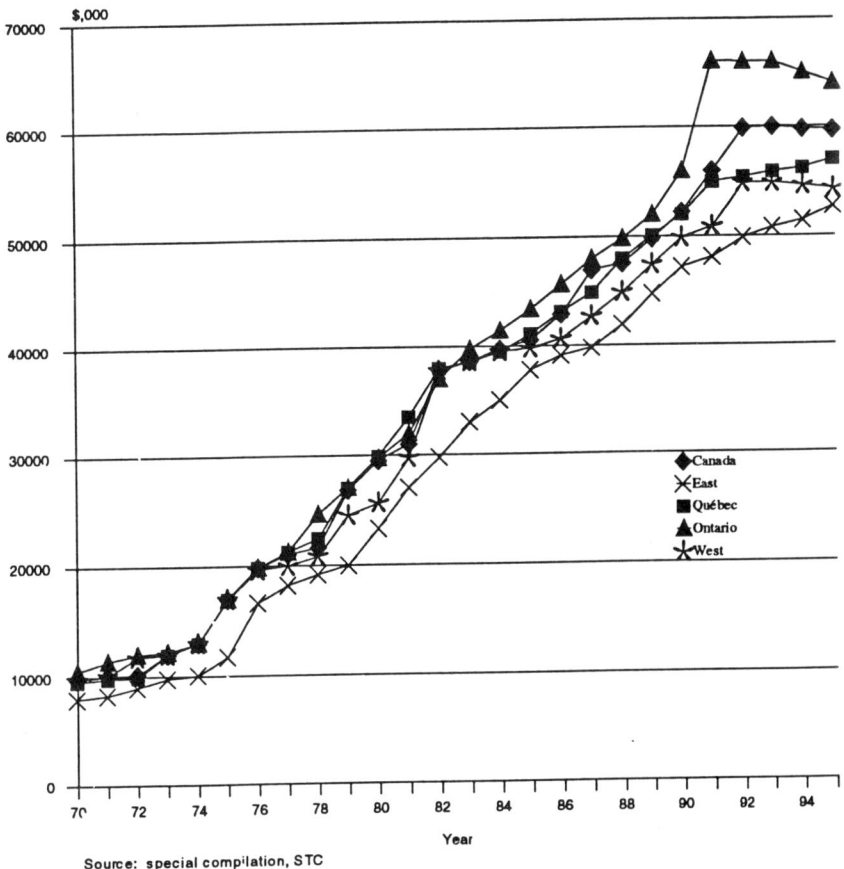

Source: special compilation, STC

Figure 6: Average Salary of Educators 1970 to 1995

As the baby boomers entered schools during the 1960s, many new teachers were hired to cope with the rapid rise in enrolment. Although enrolment levelled off in 1970 and declined thereafter, the number of educators continued to increase until 1976. This number then dropped slightly for eight years, but at a slower pace than enrolment. In 1985, the number of educators began to grow again (mainly in Ontario – because of the new financing for grades 11, 12, and 13 in Roman Catholic schools) and faster than enrolment. As these two trends moved in opposite directions, the students per educator ratio gradually decreased, from a high of 21 in 1970 to 16 by 1995 (Figure 7). The overall increase in Canada's financing effort for education during the period under review can be attributed mainly to this drop in students per educator ratio.

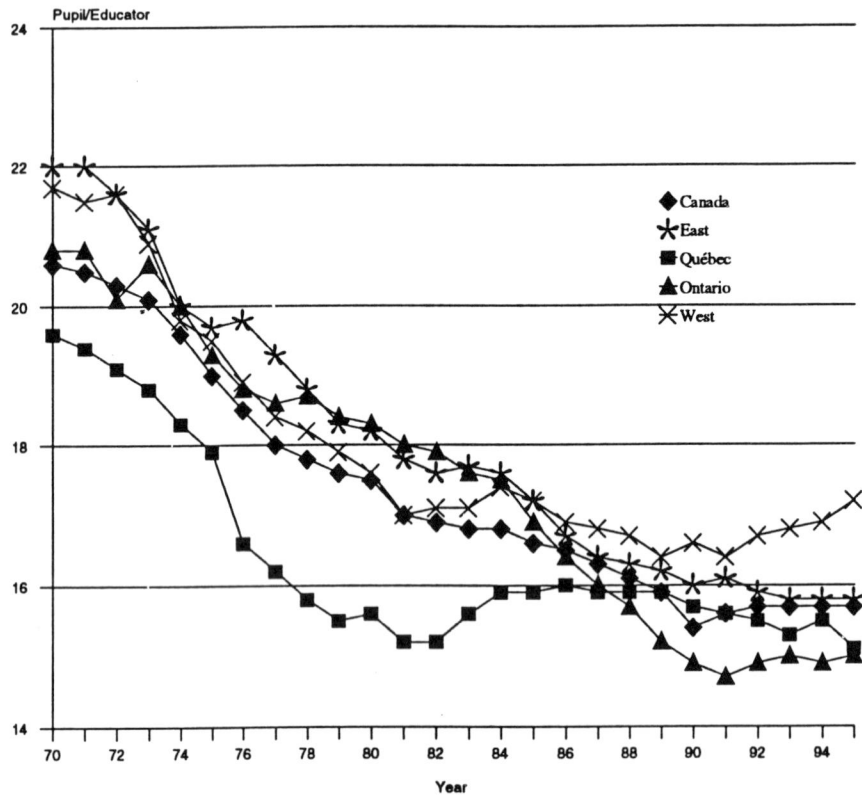

Source: special compilation, STC

Figure 7: Student-Educator Ratio 1970 to 1995

Contractual job security clauses and a school enrolment often distributed over large geographic areas prevented school administrators and governments from quickly adjusting the size of their teaching forces to the number of students. Furthermore, new educational programs were added to school curricula, including the early 1970s launch of the federal government's Official Languages in Education program. French immersion classes and second language education programs were created in all provinces, causing increased demand for new teachers. Special education programs and mainstreaming were also introduced, reducing average class size.

A look at regional variations indicates that the financing effort from Quebec and the Eastern region was above the national average during the period under study. Major cuts in Quebec teachers' salaries in 1982 and an increased workload reversed the upward trend and brought Quebec's figures in line with the national average by the end of the 1980s.[7] Overall, the financing effort for education increased in all regions (up 6.4 percentage points in Quebec, 6.2 in the East, 5.6 Ontario and 3.6 in the West.) At the national level, the increase was five percentage points, a growth of almost 25% during the whole period.

The Demographic Factor

The age structure of the general population is another important influence on education costs. For instance, a younger population means more students to educate and relatively fewer people in the labor force to support education costs. As noted earlier, the Canadian education system experienced a period of rapid expansion, at the beginning of the period under study, to an unprecented influx of baby-boomers who were aging. By 1995, the bulk of the baby-boomers were between the age of 30 and 50 and one would expect that this situation should translate into less money needed for education and more for other sectors, for example, health.

The proportion of the population aged 5 to 19,[8] the usual school-age group, diminished rapidly from 1970 to 1995 (Figure 8). From a high of 31% in 1970, the 5 to 19 age group represented only 20% of the total population by 1995. The decline was most pronounced in the 1970s and the early 1980s when the

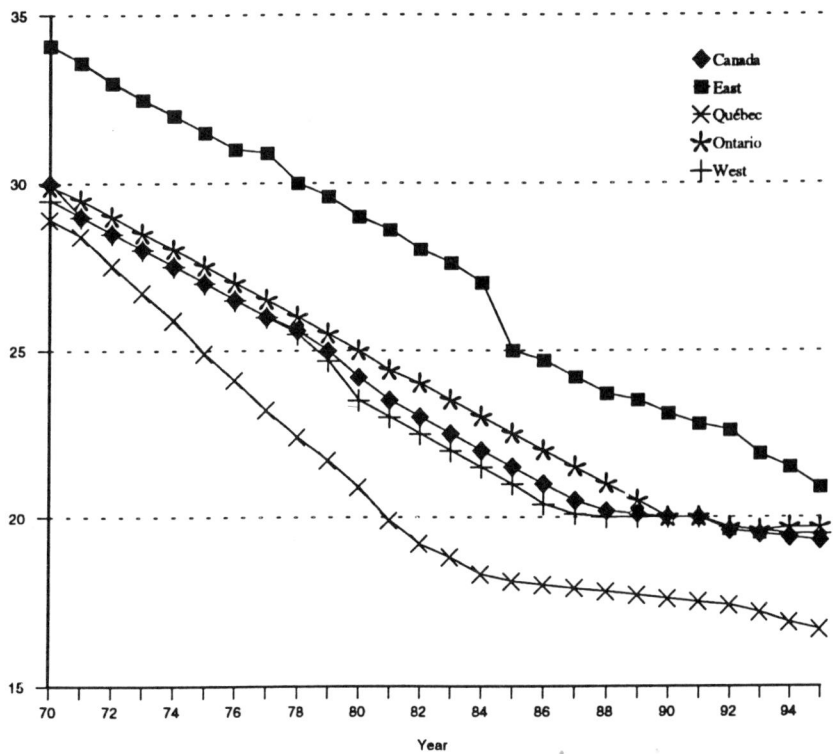

Source: Demography Division, Statistics Canada
* Population aged 5-17 for Québec

Figure 8: Proportion of Population Aged 5 to 19 to Total Population, 1970 to 1995

baby boomers gradually left school. This proportion stabilized in the 1980s and early 1990s and, according to population projections, it should remain within the 20% range until the year 2000 and decrease slightly thereafter to a low of 17% by 2016.

In theory, the decrease in the 5 to 19 age group from 1970 to 1995 should have brought reduced costs in the education sector. In a strict sense, savings were generated but they were indirectly re-invested in the system through the lowering of the students to educator ratios as explained earlier. It is estimated that if the students to educator ratios, and thus the financing effort, had remained at their 1970 level,[9] the decrease in total spending per GDP would have been much larger than what was observed. In fact, it would have stood at 3.7% in 1995 ($28.8 billion instead of $35.2 billion) and Canada would have been more in line with the OECD average rather than being among the top three countries.

In other words, the substantial reduction in school enrolment (caused by a decline in the 5 to 19 age group) was not followed by equal reductions in the number of educators and infrastructure costs. In fact, the decrease in the proportion of the school-age population was almost entirely offset by a combined increase in the financing effort and participation factors (See Figure 9).

	Canada (%)	East (%)	Quebec (%)	Ontario (%)	West (%)
Spending as a proportion of GDP, 1970	5.5	6.5	6.4	5.0	5.1
Spending as a proportion of GDP, 1995	4.6	5.1	4.5	4.7	4.2
Change 1971-1991 de 1970 à 1995	-0.9	-1.4	-1.9	-0.3	-0.9
Due to:					
Financing effort	+1.2	+1.4	+1.3	+1.3	+0.8
Demography	-2.2	-2.8	-2.9	-2.0	-1.8
Participation	+0.1	+0.0	-0.3	+0.4	+0.1

Figure 9: Contribution to Change in Spending Per GDP

Since the proportion of the 5 to 19 age group will stabilize (or even decrease in the next 15 to 20 years) and a large number of educators will reach retirement age, it is expected that governments should have more flexibility in adjusting the size of their teaching forces to more closely reflect enrolment levels.

A look at regional variations shows that during the period, the population in the Eastern region was proportionately younger than in the rest of the country. Not surprisingly, this region also had the highest student/educator ratio. By 1995, the proportions of the 5 to 19 age group were within 2% of the national average for all regions except Quebec. The two regions where demography had the greatest effect on reducing spending per student were Quebec and the East; the other two regions were below the national level of -2.2%.

The Participation Factor

The participation rate also influences spending because increased participation means more students and more educators. This is an even greater determinant at the postsecondary level since college and university education is not compulsory and participation fluctuates significantly depending on job market conditions and other personal reasons.[10] With respect to primary and secondary education, all provincial Education Acts require children aged 6 to 16 to attend school, and the participation rate for this age group is close to 100%. A look at school enrolment by age distribution in 1992-3 indicates that 91% of 5 year-olds were attending some form of pre-compulsory schooling. Also, 71%, 36%, and 11% of the population aged 17, 18, and 19 respectively, were still completing their secondary school education. Overall, the proportion of the 5 to 19 age group enrolled in primary and secondary education in 1995-6 was more than 90%.[11]

This proportion fluctuated during the 25-year period, declining steadily during the 1970s, from 89% in 1970 to 83% by the end of the decade (Figure 10). In the 1980s, the proportion increased to 88%, a sharp increase given that this ratio is affected mostly by the participation of children aged 5, 17, 18, and 19. The increase in the 1980s was partly due to more parents sending their 5 year olds to kindergarten as double-income families became more common. Also contributing to the increased participation rate during the last few years was the greater number of high school students remaining in school. Advertising campaigns stressing the importance of staying in school and graduating, and few job opportunities played a major role in this respect. The rise in spending as a proportion of GDP caused by the notable increase in participation was small compared with the importance of the financing effort (See Figure 9).

Although participation rates followed similar patterns across Canada from 1970 to 1995, it is worth noting that Quebec was the only province to record an overall decrease in participation, from 94% in 1970 to 89% in 1995. Quebec participation rates were the highest in Canada up to the late 80s. Thereafter, Ontario has taken the first place, mainly due to increased access in pre-primary education programs.

Summary

Decreased spending as a proportion of GDP observed from 1970 to 1995 in the primary and secondary education sector was entirely attributable to the significant decline in the school-age population and would have been much larger if governments had adjusted their teaching forces to reflect declining enrolment. But fixed costs and job security clauses often prevented governments from aligning costs with decreasing demand. Furthermore, the variety of programs was expanded to include, for example, French immersion and French as a second language. More importantly, the students to educator ratios dropped significantly. This drop in the students to educator ratios means higher costs since the same number of educators have been teaching to a declining number of students.

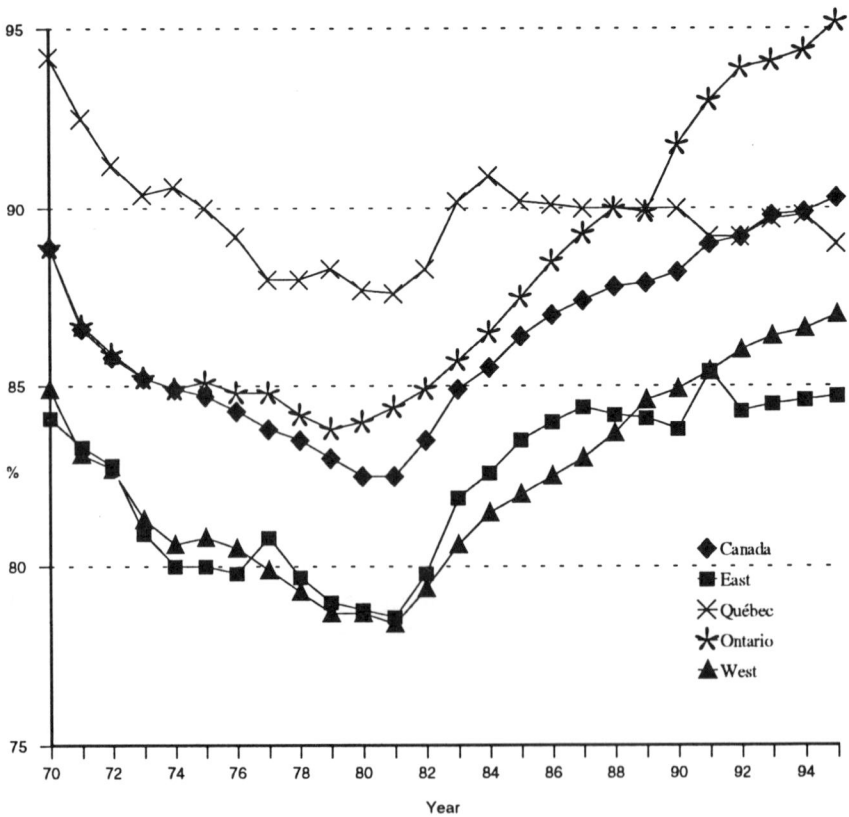

Source: special compilation, STC

*Population aged 5-17 for Québec

Figure 10: Participation Rate of School-aged Population, 1970 to 1995

If the students to educator ratios, and thus the financing effort, had remained at their 1970 level, spending on education as a proportion of GDP would have been 3.7% in 1995 – meaning Canada would have spent $6.4 billion less of its $35.5 billion budget allocated to education. Spending at the 1970 rate would have placed Canada more in line with the OECD average.

As the proportion of the 5 to 19 age group will stabilize (or even decrease in the next 15 to 20 years) and a large number of educators will reach retirement age, it is expected that governments should have more flexibility in adjusting the size of their teaching forces to closely reflect enrolment levels.

Notes

[1] See References.

[2] International comparisons are taken from Education at a Glance, OECD Indicators, Organization for Economic Co-operation and Development, 1995.

[3] This analysis looks at total expenditures on primary and secondary education, including operating and capital expenditures of public, private and special schools; ministerial expenditures (for inspection, examination, curriculum development, textbooks and so on); government contributions to teachers' superannuation plans and other federal and provincial administrative costs. GDP measures the value of all goods and services – including education services – produced in a country in a given year.

[4] In this article, "educator" includes all school-based teaching and non-teaching academic staff: classroom and resource teachers, principals, vice-principals, department heads, and school board-based instructional staff.

[5] See also "Are Higher Costs Driving Spending on Education Up? Correcting a Common Fallacy," by Diane Meaghan and Francois Casas, published in the April 1994 issue of the Canadian Education Association Newsletter. Using date from the Education Price Index published by Statistics Canada, the authors examined the cost of education relative to the cost of living, and concluded that the increase in expenditures cannot be linked to excessive increases in the cost of educational services or in the rates of remuneration for educators.

[6] Calculated as the number of full-time educators plus part-time educators in full-time equivalent.

[7] For more details about Quebec, please consult Education Indicators for the Primary and Secondary Levels, 1995, Ministere de l'Education du Quebec, 1996.

[8] The age group 5 to 17 was chosen for Quebec as most students enter the college system at age 18.

[9] It is not suggested here that the 1970 financing level would be more suitable. A look at education financing in countries of comparable size could, however, provide a basis for comparison.

[10] See "Increases in University Enrolment: Increased Access or Increased Retention?" by D.J. Lynd, Education Quarterly Review, Vol.1, No. 1 (1994). Statistics Canada, Catalogue no. 81-003.

[11] See also A Statistical Portrait of Elementary-Secondary Education in Canada, Canadian Education Statistics Council, 1992.

Data Sources

Education data were obtained from the Education, Culture and Tourism Division at Statistics Canada. Data for 1994-95 and 1995-96 are estimates and contain imputations by the author. Population data were obtained from the Demography Division at Statistics Canada. Economic data were obtained from the National Accounts and Environment Division at Statics Canada.

References

Canadian Federation of Independent Business, Skills for the Future (1989): *Small business and training in Canada.* Toronto: ON.

Canadian Labour Market and Productivity Centre (1990), "Report of the task forces on the labour market development strategy," Ottawa, ON

DesLauriers, Robert C. (1990), "The impact of employee illiteracy on Canadian business," Conference Board of Canada, Human Resources Development Centre, Ottawa, ON.

Easton, Stephen T. (1988). *Education in Canada-An analysis of elementary, secondary, and vocational schooling* Vancouver, BC: The Fraser Institute.

Economic Council of Canada (1982). A lot to learn, education, and training in Canada.

Goodlad, John I (1984). *A place called school: Prospects for the future.* New York, NY: McGraw-Hill.

L'emploi au futur: tertiarisation et polarisation, rapport de synthèse du Conseil economique du Canada (1990).

Minister of Supply and Services. Learning Well . . .Living well, the prosperity initiative, Canada 1991.

Minister of Supply and Services Canada. Federal and Provincial Support to Post-Secondary Education in Canada, A Report to Parliament, 1990-91.

Ministre de la Main-d'oeuvre, de la Sécurite du revenu et de la Formation Professionelle du Quebec (1989). Partners for People: A human Resource Adjustment and Development Strategy for the 1990s.

Ministre des Approvisionnements et Services Canada. Batir ensemble l'avenir du Canada, 1991.

National Centre on Education and the Economy (1990). America's Choice: High Skills or Low Wages, Report of the Commission on the Skills of the American Workforce.

Nous accomplir: apprendre pour l'avenir, Forum entreprises-universites (1991)

Ontario Government (1990). *People and skills in the new global economy,. A report by the Premier's Council.* Toronto, ON: Queen's Printer for Ontario.

Organization de cooperation et de developpement economiques. L'education et l'economie dans une societe en mutation, (1989)

Porter, Michael E. (1989, 1990) *The competitive advantage of nations,* New York, NY The Free Press

U.S. Department of Labor (1989). Investing in people: A strategy to address America's work force crisis, A report to the Secretary of Labor, Commission on Work Force Quality and Labor Market Efficiency.

2

The Impact of Changes in Federal Provincial Block Transfers
Dan Perrins

Introduction

The replacement of the Established Programs Financing (EPF) arrangement by the new Canada Health and Social Transfer (CHST) was a key element of the 1995 federal budget. The CHST has been in effect since April 1, and it is still too soon to know the full extent of the ramifications of the change, and of other changes in the budget with implications for post-secondary education and training, but enough information is available to make some informed speculations.

It is now evident that reductions in federal transfer payments under the CHST have caused – and likely will continue to cause – serious difficulties for provincial finance ministers as they attempt to maintain balanced budgets or momentum towards that goal. But the CHST is not the only federal change with a huge fiscal impact. Another is the creation of the Human Resources Investment Fund (HRIF) and the effects on job-training and adult basic education. While my remarks today will focus on the CHST, I don't want to neglect the very direct and potentially devastating effects of the HRIF and EI changes on colleges and technical institutes across Canada.

I propose to address the changes in federal transfers by, first, reviewing the history of federal involvement in the funding of post-secondary education, then by reviewing the changes made as a result of the 1995 Federal Budget and, finally, by offering my assessment of some likely consequences of the changes.

History of Federal Funding of Post-Secondary Education

Of course, education is a provincial responsibility under our Constitution. Nonetheless, the federal government has had a role in funding post-secondary education – university education, in particular – for more than half a century. The Youth Training Act of 1939 made loans and scholarships available to university students. With huge numbers of soldiers about to be demobilized, the 1945 Veterans Rehabilitation Act offered grants to war veterans to assist them in attending university and allowed for direct grants to universities in recognition of the bulge in student numbers caused by the large veteran enrolment. Direct grants continued even after the veterans had completed their studies, in line with the recommendations from the 1951 Massey Royal Commission. The technical and Vocational Assistance Act of 1960 recognized the growing importance of technical training by instituting a cost-sharing program in support of vocational and technical training. The Canada Student Loan Plan was introduced in 1964.

The modern era of significant federal presence in post-secondary education is often marked by the 1967 Federal-Provincial Fiscal Arrangements Acts, which replaced direct grants to universities by cash transfers and tax-point transfers to provincial governments. Under this act, university operating expenditures were shared equally by the federal and provincial governments. This arrangement lasted for ten years, until 1977, when the EPF (Established Programs Financing) was instituted. Under EPF, the federal government provided block funding to the provinces, but the amounts were tied to provincial population figures, not to university expenditures. While per-capita EPF payments were to increase in relation to the growth in the Gross National Product, these annual adjustments were capped or frozen at least eight times during the EPF's lifetime.

The Mechanics of EPF

It may be worthwhile to digress briefly at this point to review the structure of EPF transfers. In the decade prior to 1977, the federal government paid one-half of all post-secondary and health expenditures in Canada – though, interestingly, this 50-50 sharing occurred only on a total basis, not province by province. Partly to achieve equity from one province to the next, and partly to restrict the ability of provincial governments to dictate federal expenditures by increasing their expenditures of "50-cent dollars," the EPF program was introduced. Under EPF, each province received the same per-capita transfer from Ottawa each year.

The EPF transfer payments had two components: a tax-point transfer and a cash transfer. The tax-point transfer occurred in 1977 when the federal government reduced both personal and corporate income taxes, allowing the provinces to increase their income tax rates so that total tax receipts were roughly constant. The value of the tax points was set so as to generate one-half of the pre-EPF federal payments in respect of health and post-secondary education. The cash payments were also set a one-half of the pre-EPF transfers, so that the initial EPF transfers maintained federal support at the pre-EPF level of the 1976 fiscal year.

Originally, the plan was for the revenues generated by the tax-point transfer and the cash transfers to grow independently of another. The cash payments were intended to increase in relation to growth in the Gross National Product and the tax-corporate incomes in a particular province. However, in 1982, the EPF rules were changed to put a ceiling on total EPF transfers. Since then an annual per-capita EPF transfer amount has been calculated, and each province has received in cash the amount by which the per-capita EPF payment exceeded the estimated per-capita revenue accruing to that province from the tax-point transfer. Additional restrictions on EPF payments have been made at least half a dozen times since then. Figure 1 illustrates the breakdown of EPF allocations for each province during the 1992-93 fiscal year, as calculated by the federal government.

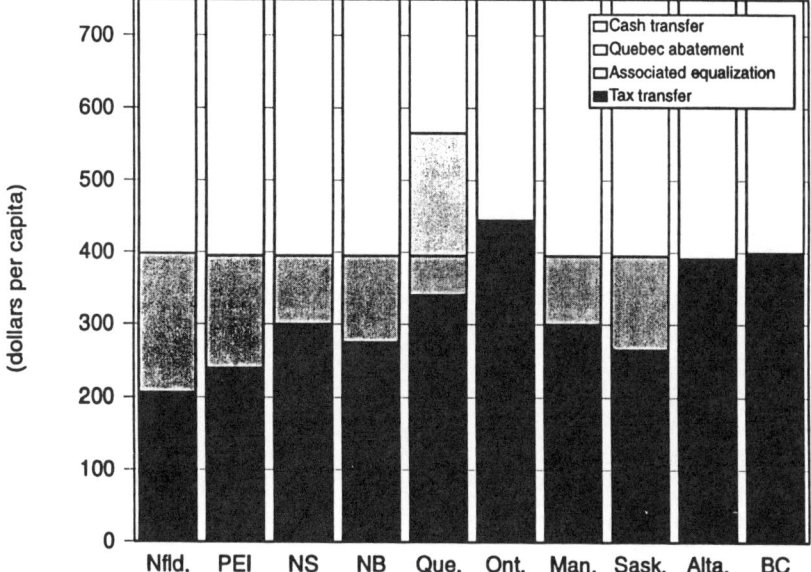

Source: Courchene[1], page 115.

Figure 1: How Established Programs Financing Works, fiscal year 1992-93.

Some other points should be mentioned in this connection. First, while the federal government considered the whole per-capita EPF amount to be a transfer payment, the only flow of money from Ottawa to the provinces occurred by virtue of the cash transfers. The revenues collected as a result of the tax-point transfer already flowed directly into provincial coffers.

Second, because 32.1% of federal transfers before EPF supported post-secondary education, the federal government has consistently allocated a nominal 32.1% of EPF transfers to post-secondary education and 67.9% to health care. The provinces have not accepted this breakdown, especially since total expenditures on health care now exceed those on post-secondary education by far more than the 2 to 1 ratio suggested by the federal government's allocation. Indeed, the change in the ratio of provincial spending on health to spending on post-secondary education which is now more than 5 to 1 in Saskatchewan – occurred in part because federal actions, such as the Canada Health Act, effectively forced a shift in provincial spending priorities. This shift in priorities led to reductions in the proportion of provincial expenditures devoted to post-secondary education, at a time when enrolments were climbing rapidly. Even though their operating grants continued to rise during the 1980s and into the 1990s, post-secondary institutions have often struggled during the past decade to find the necessary resources to maintain their arrays of programs and services.

Finally, it should be noted that Quebec's notional EPF transfers had a third component to take into account a tax abatement that Quebec, alone amongst the provinces, had accepted in the late 1960s.

Those interested in more information about EPF are referred to pages 108-117 of Courchene.

The 1995 Federal Budget

Perhaps the most widely-known provision of the 1995 budget is the Canada Health and Social Transfer (Government of Canada, 1995), which replaced both EPF and the Canada Assistance Plan (CAP). In fact, the CHST has hogged much of the limelight, but the 1995 Federal Budget contained other provisions with serious consequences for post-secondary education. Changes to unemployment insurance legislation – though the proposed EI program – mean that the federal government will buy fewer seats in job-training programs at technical institutions and community colleges, thus causing a significant decline in revenues for those institutions. The creation of the Human Resources Investment Fund (HRIF) will lead to reduced funding for apprenticeship programs and adult basic education. Finally, the budgets of the major research granting agencies – the Medical Research Council, the Natural Sciences and Engineering Research Council and the Social Sciences and Humanities Research Council – have been cut by about 14% over three years. These cuts will force university researchers to reduce their research activities or else find alternative funding.

Under the CHST, the federal government now makes a lump-sum payment to each province as a federal contribution towards the costs of health care, social services and post-secondary education. Of course, a critical component of the change is the reduction of $2.8 billion during the current year, as compared to combined CAP and EPF payments last year, with another $1.8 billion scheduled to take effect for 1997-98. This amounts to a cumulative reduction in excess of 15% from 1995-96 federal transfers under EPF and CAP, including tax-point transfers. Since cuts all will come out of the cash transfers, the proportional drop in new cash received by the provinces will be much higher; for example, Saskatchewan is expecting its federal cash transfers under CHST, to drop by a third over the two-year period. Further, the 1996 Federal Budget proposed to freeze CHST cash payments at about $11 billion (including the Quebec tax abatement) until the end of fiscal year 2000, and then to raise them gradually until the fiscal year 2003. The decline in federal support for social programs is illustrated in Figure 2, which shows the anticipated CHST payments, net of Quebec tax abatement, until 2003. Since CHST payments will reflect provincial population numbers, the provinces which are growing the most rapidly will gain a larger share of the $11 billion, at the expense of the other provinces.

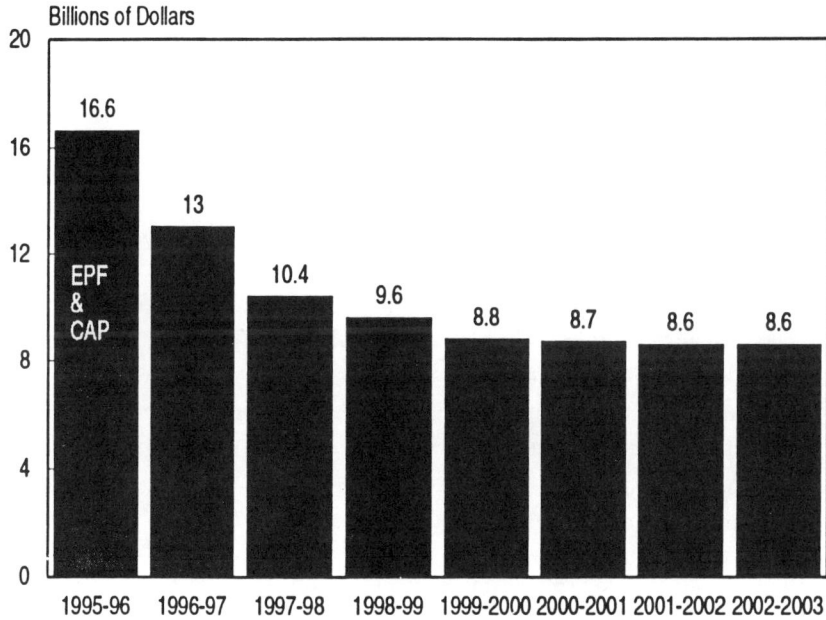

*Cash transfers do not include the amount of the Quebec Abatement

Source: Federal Finance

Figure 2: CHST Cash Transfers* to All Provinces and Territories

The CHST legislation preserves the requirement that provincial medicare and health plans maintain the five principles of the Canada Health Act: universality, portability, public administration, accessibly, and no extra-billing or user fees. The CHST also requires provinces to continue to ensure that social services are available to all residents, regardless of how long they lived in the province, but the other principles underlying CAP (appealing process, needs-based services, and public administration) have been discarded. Neither CHST nor EPF enunciates principles governing post-secondary services. The federal government, however, has expressed a willingness to negotiate additional principles to govern health, social services and post-secondary education with the provinces.

Most detailed descriptions and assessments of the CHST are available; see, for example, Courdhene (1996) or Mendelson (1996).

Enhanced Role for the Provinces in Post-Secondary Education

There is one simple consequence of the changes ensuing from the 1995 Federal Budget: in the future, the federal government will spend less money in support of post-secondary education and research than it has in the past. This means that the provinces and beneficiaries will bear a much larger responsibility for funding post-secondary education than been the case over the past thirty years.

The big question then, is: How will the provinces manage change? No doubt, there will be no single answer to this question. In a general sense, each province has three options:

(a) to shield its post-secondary institutions completely from the effects of the federal cutbacks, as British Columbia has done this year;

(b) to backfill the federal reductions partially, while spreading out the remainder of the federal cuts across the rest of government, as Saskatchewan (1996) has done;

(c) to off-load virtually the full impact of the federal reductions onto the post-secondary institutions, as Ontario apparently intends to do.

Whatever approaches the various provinces choose, it is clear that the reductions in federal transfer payments will have profound effects on education in Canada. While it is too early to make definitive statements about the nature of these changes, some likely trends are emerging.

Stronger provincial role in post-secondary education.

While the provinces have never surrendered their constitutional right to determine the shape of their respective education systems, the provinces have arguably taken a national perspective – or, at least, they have avoided parochial perspectives – on post-secondary education. This is particularly evident in provinces like Saskatchewan, which has long been an exporter of university graduates. As the federal presence in the funding of post-secondary education declines, it is likely that provincial needs will play an increasingly dominant role in shaping teaching and research programs at post-secondary institutions.

A greater provincial focus raises some troubling questions. For example, there is already wide-spread concern that the universities are graduating "too many" lawyers, nurses, and teachers. Should admissions to professional programs be determined by the number of professionals needed in a particular province? Or, instead, should the universities attempt to accommodate the continued strong demand for such programs? Some will argue that it is a waste of scarce resources to educate students for professions in which they are unlikely to find employment upon graduation, and that it is unfair to the students to "lead them on" by admitting them to such programs, only to be disappointed when the hoped-for lucrative positions fail to materialize after they graduate. Others will argue that a society should strive to provide as broad an array of educational options as possible and should not deny access to certain programs because of job-market uncertainties. Reconciling these viewpoints will be difficult, if not impossible. But, as the provincial role in funding post-secondary institutions grows, it will not be surprising if more parochial approaches prevail over time.

A related issue concerns university research. Since provincial operating grants pay for non-sponsored research and for indirect costs of funded research, the provinces may be tempted to try to dictate the direction and focus of research, at their universities. After all, if the province is paying, why should not the researchers direct their efforts towards provincial priorities? To a certain extent, this argument has some merit. Moreover, any university that ignores this argument does so at its own peril; by using its research capacity to solve important provincial problems, a university proves its worth to the public and thereby engenders greater support for its research work. However, there is danger in taking this approach too far. Many of the great inventions of the Twentieth Century (e.g. penicillin, transistors, lasers, computer chips) were the result of research or curiosity-based solutions to current practical problems. It should be mentioned, too, that universities operate in national and international environments, and so it is important not to let the universities get too far out of step with their counterparts elsewhere.

There will be less (or different) accessibility

Constrained funding for post-secondary institutions will inevitably affect accessibility. Some effects are obvious. For example, if a university closes a department or college or faculty, access is immediately reduced for students who live near that university. Similarly, tuition fees will increase to cover some of the shortfall in operating grants, and those fee increases will induce some students to take fewer classes, thereby lengthening their programs, or to drop out altogether.

Other effects are more subtle. Reduced provincial support may translate into a scaling-back, but not the elimination, of some programs. In this case, students wanting access to the affected programs would face stiffer competition for admission. It is worth noting, though, that accessibility will remain a high priority for governments – and for the universities, since high enrolments enhance their status, reinforce funding arguments and raise needed revenues through tuition fees. But universities may seek alternative means of maintaining access.

Different delivery systems will come into use

Fiscal stringency will likely lead to a heavier emphasis on new and different means of delivering programs, which in turn would lead enhance or maintain accessibility. These changes could take a number of forms.

One approach involves greater use of multimedia approaches to deliver programs off-campus. There is a great deal of interest in multimedia approaches these days. There will be significant up-front costs, and a multimedia approach may be much more suitable to some programs than others, but recent technological advances make multimedia strategies attractive in the current environment.

Another approach involves the organization of program delivery. Most post-secondary programs are offered in traditional lecture formats on campus., under the auspices of the institutions which sponsor the programs. We may see a trend towards a more co-operative approach to program delivery through the sharing of resources. For example, the recent formation of a consortium of the universities in Halifax calls for a sharing of programs and faculty, providing students with increased access and greater mobility. In Saskatchewan, some have suggested the creation of regional centres. which would control of the offering of post-secondary – and perhaps even elementary and secondary – programs within their respective regions.

K-12 Systems Will be Affected.

The consequences of the reductions in the federal transfer payments on elementary and secondary education will be indirect, but very real. The need for provincial governments to rescale their spending patterns to accommodate the federal cuts will likely lead to somewhat reduced funding for K-12 systems, except in cases where governments decide to off-load the whole federal reduction onto their health-care, social services and post-secondary sectors. Even then, there would likely be demands for greater efficiencies and new ways of doing things in all departments, including education.

The K-12 systems will probably be affected indirectly in at least two ways. First, since the means of delivering post-secondary programs will change and accessibility may be reduced, there will be consequences for graduating high school students as they attempt to move into post-secondary studies or into the work force. As post-secondary delivery systems change, the high schools will have to ensure that their graduates are positioned to take maximum advantage of the new approaches. If accessibility is reduced, there could be demands on the high schools' resources as Grade 12 graduates return to attempt to upgrade their marks.

The second indirect effect of the federal cuts on the k-12 systems could involve curriculum development. Traditionally, the provinces have jealously guarded their control over curricula in their schools. However, the funding crunch ensuing from the decline in federal transfer payments may cause some provinces to develop curriculum changes together, if only for cost-effectiveness. In fact, some interprovincial co-operation in the development of mathematics curriculum is currently under way in the four western provinces.

Serious Potential for Labor Relations Problems.

Many post-secondary institutions have already laid off support staff and administrative staff – and this was before the federal cutbacks! It has been evident ever since the 1995 Federal Budget that the budget was increasing nervousness about job security, even amongst tenured university faculty, since closures of programs, departments or institutions would inevitably mean lay-offs of faculty. Unions representing elementary and high school teachers have already signalled their unhappiness with cut-backs to the K-12 systems. Employer-union relationships will be delicate until the federal cuts have been absorbed.

The country will be changed.

Over the past forty or so years, post-secondary education has expanded to accommodate increasing numbers of students and demands from society for other services. The federal government has been an integral part of the process, through its direct and indirect support of post-secondary institutions. The federal government cannot suddenly withdraw a great deal of its financial support without causing a sea change in attitudes and the availability of post-secondary education. The timing of the federal pull-back is problematic too, since projections suggest that Canada will need more, not fewer, post-secondary graduated and that demands for post-secondary education will increase, not decrease, in the years to come.

The expansion phase engendered a national perspective towards post-secondary education and a recognition of the importance of accessibility as a means to help citizens achieve their full potential. As the federal cutbacks take effect, it is likely (and understandable) that more parochial attitudes will prevail. After all, the provinces will inherit the lion's share of the responsibility for funding post-secondary education, and it will be argued that provincial funding should support, in the main, provincial priorities. Rather than taking a national, or even international attitude towards the labor market, people may ask why their provincial government is spending scarce tax-dollars to educate or train students who move to other provinces or other countries. A question like this goes against the once-prevalent attitude that citizens should have a wide variety of career options. But questions like this are often heard nowadays, even in Saskatchewan, which has traditionally been a net exporter of post-secondary graduates.

Conclusion

Most people accept that government deficits are a problem and must be dealt with — and that reducing those deficits will cause some pain. Even those who don't accept this proposition must face the fact that the federal cuts in support of the social safety net are now law and must be accommodated. This means that tough decisions have to be made, but it is essential that short-term priorities not be allowed to cloud the long-term viability of post-secondary institutions and programs.

Canada post-secondary institutions, especially universities, have been making important contributions to the economic, social, and technological well-being of this country for well over a century. In addition to their teaching programs, these institutions have provided a wide variety of services to their communities and, though research programs, have chalked up some significant advances in medicine, agriculture and a host of other areas. In our zeal to reshape and revitalize our post-secondary systems, we must take care not to harm the capacity of these institutions to continue to make such contributions. Once removed, a teaching or research program would not easily be restored.

In my view, a system wide perspective is critical in reconfiguring post-secondary education in Canada in the wake of the federal cutbacks. This perspective can have a provincial focus. Governments and institutions can work together to define provincial needs and priorities, and then proceed to devise the most effective means of achieving those needs. This may entail some program closures or mergers – as we have seen in Nova Scotia – but the short-term upheaval would be worth the while if the end result is a more effective post-secondary system, making the best possible use of scarce resources.

A regional and national perspective is also essential. This could take very specific forms, such as agreements between provinces to offer certain high-cost, low-enrolment programs jointly, on a regional basis; the Western College of Veterinary Medicine at the University of Saskatchewan, jointly funded by the four western provinces, is one example. But a regional or national perspective would also include a genuine concern for the needs and priorities of the country as a whole when program decisions are taken.

References

Courchene, Thomas J. (1994). *Social Canada in the millenium: Reform imperatives and restructuring principles.* Toronto, ON: C.D. Howe Institute.

Courchene, Thomas J. (1996). *Redistributing money and power: A guide to the Canada health and social transfer.* Toronto, ON: C.D. Howe Institute.

Government of Canada, Budget papers, 1995.

Government of Saskatchewan, Budget papers, 1996.

Government of Canada, Budget papers, 1996.

Mendelson, Michael (1996). *Looking for Mr.good-transfer: A guide to the CHST negotiations.* Caledon Institute of Social Policy.

3

School Reforms and Financial Considerations:

A Policy Analysis

Y.L. Jack Lam

Introduction

For those interested in recent development in the Canadian public education, they will note there are two important trends that tend to be coexist side by side in almost every province. The first common trend, reflected in various government documents, such as *Renewing Education: New Directions* (Manitoba Department of Education and Training, 1995) and *Education Horizons* (Nova Scotia Department of Education, 1995), which outline the new thrusts various provincial governments use to reform their school systems. The second common trend is the notable funding reduction, downsizing and consolidation of school jurisdictions (Manitoba School Divisions/Districts Boundaries Review Commission, 1994; Ontario School Board Reduction Task Force, 1996, as examples) in their separate efforts of reducing budget deficits.

The intriguing question one needs to ask is: To what extent are these trends related to each other? If these are related, a follow-up question to be raised is : How do financial considerations influence the proposed school reforms and changes? There are a few ways to search for solutions to these questions. However, the analysis of government policies should provide the most direct approach of identifying the answers.

The meaning of "policy" and its related "policy research" have been fairly ambiguous (Guthrie, 1977). And yet, policy analysis is one of the most fascinating and fast growing research endeavor. Over the last few decades, it has expanded into the disciplines like economics, sociology, political science, law and education. Such a popularity is rested on its intimate relationship with the social values that shape our judgment, color our perspective and guide our actions.

While we might like to see that policy development is influenced by expert opinions and accomplished by public participatory decision-making (MacIver, 1990), policy development is never a rational process. It is, very often, an outcome of competing interest groups articulating certain social values and putting pressure on the governing authority to decree policies (Downey, 1988) that enhance self-preservation. There are times, as the present situation tends to show, when the governing authority has a certain definitive agenda, it tends to align itself with groups sharing its visions and interests and brushes aside those that have a dissimilar agenda. Furthermore, to ensure its agenda will not be unduly disrupted, the governing authority will entrench its course of actions in legislative acts with clauses that heighten its power of control.

To test these hypotheses, the present chapter focuses on the analysis of a group of education bills that were recently passed by Manitoba. The choice of Manitoba should not be viewed primarily as a provincial matter. Rather, as alluded earlier, given the similarities of agenda and purposes of all levels of Governments in Canada, the analysis of what a provincial government does should reflect national tendency and attain national significance.

The Stage

In the fall sitting of the Manitoba legislature in 1996, the Government, by using its majority in the Legislative Assembly, manifested its resolve to pass a series of educational bills. Earlier testing of the water by the government through its routine consultation process, revealed that the various reports upon which these bills were based were highly controversial and incited much fear and opposition from the teaching profession. Yet, to compromise or to accommodate the concerns of the professional educators would deviate the government from its charted course.

Two main strategies were subsequently adopted by the Government. The first was to delay the most controversial components of the bills for later legislative consideration. Included in this category were proposed changes in teacher salary classification, recertification and incentive pays (Dyck, Render & Carlyle, 1995), and school divisions/districts consolidation (Manitoba School Divisions/Districts Boundaries Review Commission, 1994). The second inter-related strategy was to pass speedily those bills that received support from some provincial interest groups. To meet this end, the Government has taken the unprecedented move of restricting the debate time in the Legislative Assembly while allowing the public hearing to go through its "democratic rituals" after the second reading of the bills.

The bills that were rushed through include the following:

a. Bill 26, The Labour Relations Amendment Act

b. Bill 32, The Council on Post-secondary Education Act;

c. Bill 33, The Education Administration Amendment Act;

d. Bill 47(1), The Public Schools Amendment Act;

e. Bill 51, The Civil Service Superannuation Amendment, Public Servants Insurance Amendment and Teacher Pensions Amendment Act;

f. Bill 57, the Public Sector Compensation Disclosure Act; and,

g. Bill 72, the Public Schools Amendment Act (2).

Nature of Four of the Bills

Of these seven education and education-related bills, two may be viewed as either curtailing the power of the teachers or increasing the power of the Minister of Education (i.e. Bill 26, and Bill 33). Two are housing-keeping bills which tend to update some of the existing regulations (i.e., Bill 47 and Bill 51). Even then, in one of the house-keeping bills (Bill 47), there are some sections that deal with the financial aspects of the school board operation. The remaining three bills attempt to both enhance the power or control of the government and to restrict financial spending of the public education institutions (i.e., Bill 32, Bill 57 and Bill 72). Evidently, out of the seven bills considered here, about four contained sections of financial management that government hopes to regulate. These four bills, therefore, necessitate further scrutiny.

Bill 32

Bill 32 was intended to tighten the governance structure of universities and colleges by replacing the current loosely structured University Grants Commission with a regulatory body called the Council on Post-secondary Education, and by increasing the power of the Minister of Education for direct control.

In specifics, the Council so established will operate within the framework of accountability provided by the Minister of Education. Through the council, all priorities of the post-secondary institutions should be consistent with programs, policies and guidelines of the government. The council is further empowered to determine the level of funding, advise in the planning and delivery of academic programs, services and facilities, assist the development of a clear mandate for each post-secondary institution, develop accountability criteria for measuring their core functions of teaching, research and services, monitor and regulate financial information, establish policies for tuition fees and appoint persons or committee for review of every post-secondary institution.

Through these duties and powers of the Council, it is quite evident that the regulatory body will exert its influence on post-secondary institutions on every aspect of their operations. The traditional autonomy and freedom that universities enjoyed are sacrificed for the benefit of government's tighter control.

Explicitly and implicitly, the purpose for tighter control is to achieve greater financial economization of all post-secondary education. The wordings in Section 11 pertaining to "duties" clearly state that the council will "allocate funding to universities . . . with a view to avoid unnecessary duplication of effort and expense. . . ." To do so, section 12 indicates that the council may "require a university . . . to provide . . . financial or other information that the council considers necessary." To avoid post-secondary institutions adopting differential tuition fees which is commonly resorted to counter-balance funding shortfalls, and which generally constitute 20% of the university's total income, the council is now empowered to "establish policies" to govern how much students' fees can be or should be raised. Section 18 further stipulates that the annual funding plan submitted by post-secondary institutions should be subjected to rigorous review by the council which "shall not make any expenditure commitments that are not within the financial limits set by the annual funding plan." The final decision in funding allocation will be at the disposal of the Minister of eEucation.

Bill 47

Bill 47 is the Public Schools Amendment Act. While the intent of this bill is to update regulations that are obsolete, it does contain three sections that have financial implications for the school divisions. Section 41(5.1) states that

> where a resident pupil attends a program at a school in another school division and that program is offered by the home school division, the home school division shall pay a pupil transfer fee to the other school division in accordance with the regulations.

In the past, if the home school has offered the same program as another neighboring school division, there will be no financial support to the student when he/she opts for another division. By this regulation, the Government has explicitly encouraged competition and parental choice as one measure of retaining or upgrading program quality among school divisions, and this should have enormous financial ramification for school divisions whose programs may be deemed inferior in the eyes of the parents while comparing to others.

Sections 41(8), to 41(11) stipulate that each school board shall annually appoint an auditor to make a report to the board on annual financial statements that he/she has examined as at the end of the fiscal year. Qualification of the auditor should be complied with the authority of an Act of Legislature and the name should be submitted to the minister for approval.

Through the approved auditor, the government will be in a better position to review the financial situation of each school board. Combined with Sections 41.1(1), 41.1(2) that deals with the board's obligations related to "accumulated deficit" the government is empowered to monitor, control the financial spending and eliminate budget deficits of every school division in the Province.

Bill 57

Bill 57 is the Public Sector Compensation Discloser Act. After defining "compensation" to include "cash and non-cash salary, allowances, bonuses, commissions . . ." in Section 1 of the Act, Section 2 mandates that, "within six months after the end of each fiscal year ending on March 31, 1996, a public sector body shall disclose to the public . . . employees whose compensation is $50 000 or more." Failing to do so, according to Section 8, the minister of education may order "that an amount not exceeding 15% of the amount of funding payable by the government to a public sector body be withheld until disclosure as required by this Act has been made."

Evidently, there is no subtlety nor concealment on the part of the government to adopt in a high-handed manner what it believes to be the confidential information on every aspect of public institutions public to bring about greater accountability. There are several concerns that must be contemplated here. First of all, listing individuals (notably those with moderate to very high incomes) in public domain could trigger comparison, jealousy and hostility against the professional from the public given the current high unemployment and under-employment rates. Teachers whose salaries are in the range of $50 000, feel particularly vulnerable when they work in small, rural, remote or aboriginal communities where the general incomes are low.

By revealing the public sector body's employees' salary, it begs the question pertaining to the actual motives of the government: Is this a political device to put public opinions and pressure in place to forestall future improvement of employees' monetary compensation? or Is this a measure to ensure greater productivity for the resources channelled into the public organization? If the government's intent is for the latter, it should be considered to be the most round-about-way of achieving the objective. One needs only to refer to Bill 32 and Bill 47 to see how *direct* the government can be to accomplish "accountability." It takes little explanation for the government to regulate and control post-secondary institutions and school boards to fall in line with the government objectives of austerity. This leaves the government's motive implicit in the first question more or less intact. Argument substantiating this postulation can further be strengthened as Bill 72 is reviewed.

Bill 72

Bill 72 intends to revamp the entire process of negotiation process which becomes an annual ritual between school boards and local teacher associations. There are several major points that depart radically from the past practice.

One critical area pertains to the disclosure of relevant information to pertinent parties engaged in the negotiation as well as to the public. Falling into this category are two sections. Section 110.2(1) states that "school board shall give the bargaining agent a copy of its most recent budget and access to relevant financial information in its possession or control related to the budget." Section 128(3) further states that "information obtained from evidence, including documents or things, produced to an arbitrator . . . may be made public."

Another aspect of the Bill deals with some area of teachers' working conditions excluded from negotiation or arbitration. Specifically, Section 126(2) identifies four areas which are not referable for arbitration. These include the selection, appointment, assignment and transfer of teachers and principals; the method for evaluating the performance of teachers and principals; the size of classes in schools; and the scheduling of recesses and the mid-day break.

A further change that departs from the current negotiation process deals with the ultimate criterion an arbitrator must use in settling disputes during the negotiation. Section 129(3) indicates "the arbitrator shall, in respect of matters that might reasonably be expected to have a financial effect on the school division or school district, base his or her decision *primarily on* the school division's or school district's *ability to pay* . . ."

Evidently, by introducing these changes, the Government attempts to expedite the current collective bargaining which has been viewed as cumbersome, ineffective, time-consuming and resource-wasteful, a point well recognized by past research (for example, Hennessy, 1977; Lam, 1981; Lam & Kong, 1981). As working conditions of teachers are taking up more and more time in negotiation, the government hopes that Section 126 could narrow the scope of the issues in which teachers can negotiate.

More interestingly, by insisting that the board reveal its financial situation to the teacher association, the government hopes that teachers' demands in the salary increment should fall in line with the financial situation of the school division/district. Failing to achieve this objective, the government has provided section 110.2 for the board to disclose the information to the public hoping that pressure from the public could be used to bring salary negotiation to a closure. To ensure that the financial situation of the school board is not adversely affected when information sharing and public pressure have not been effective in curtailing the salary demands of teachers, the final assurance that the government inserts is the arbitrator assigned to resolve the dispute will have to consider the board's ability to pay as the *sole* criterion in recommending solution to the impasse.

With the exclusion of some working conditions from the bargaining process and with the restriction imposed on salary compensation, this bill has been viewed by the teacher organization as anti-union and autocratic, rendering the tractional collective bargaining process completely useless. To the government, however, this bill in conjunction with others already mentioned, will bring the expenditure for the public school completely under control, given that salary of the teaching staff constitutes approximately 77% of the provincial education budget (Manitoba Education and Training, School Finance Branch, 1992).

Common Characteristics of the Bills

Irrespective of the nature of the bills discussed, it seems self-evident that financial consideration plays a major role in shaping and wording the various provincial statutes. Control of the financial spending on the post-secondary education, the government, through Bill 32, wades into an unfamiliar territory and creates a structure to regulate all aspects of post-secondary institutions. To ensure that no school board will ever be allowed in operate in deficits, the government, through Bill 47, demands a more fiscal rigorous control over the boards' operation and make them responsible to correcting their financial positions. To assure that the professional educators should not become excessive in their demands for monetary rewards, the disclosure of individuals' salaries above $50 000 allow public pressure and opinions to act as watchdogs. This also lays the framework for ensuring that professional educators become more accountable to the public by tying educators' monetary compensation to their performance. To render greater control on monetary advancement of educators through the collective bargaining, the whole negotiation process is now governed by the sole principle of "boards' ability to pay."

A second feature common among these legislature is in all bills, the power of the government, through the minister of education, is greatly enhanced. It would seem logical to the government that to regulate all public expenditures in different levels of education, its power must be increased at the expense of the traditional practices (as in the case of negotiation), of the powerful teacher organization and of time-honored autonomous tradition of universities. In so doing, it has demonstrated its distrust in the educational community as a responsible body while trying to bring financial management in proper order.

Consequences of the Government Current Approach

While on surface, the government has achieved what it has set out to achieve, there are serious ramification for its high-handed approach in translating its agenda into public policies:

1. Inability in Creating a Common Vision

In trying to update the education legislature to coincide with the government-initiated school reform, the present Manitoba government seems to be overly obsessed with the financial concern and fiscal restraint. While this neo-conservative position is similar to what the other provincial governments and the federal government of Canada are taking in their separate attempts to balance the provincial/federal budgets and to reduce provincial/national deficits, we may suggest that the vision of the Manitoba government, as expressed through its legislation and public policies, rather than through its constant rhetoric and publicity documents, is too narrowly focused. In face of a lack of common vision with major stakeholders, and worse still, in its naked desire to regulate and control, rather than seeking consensus in school reform, the future attainment of the government's ambitious goals is at stake.

2. Damaged Government Creditability

In its rush to achieve its agenda, the government has radically departed from the participatory policy making process that it has followed in the past. The so called public hearings were primarily for show, as few major concerns expressed by various presentations have been seriously considered, and as fewer significant adjustments or modifications have ben made in the final versions of the bills. By making a mockery of the democratic consultation process, the government's creditability of accommodating diverse interests of all stakeholders is cast in doubt. In this context, the government is likely to reap the short term gains for the long term pains. Future working relationships between the government and all interest groups will be jeopardized in a prevailing atmosphere of distrust.

3. Heightened Political Tension among Special Interest Groups

Prior to the various bills becoming public policies or provincial laws, the minister did invite representatives from the Manitoba Teachers Society, Manitoba Association of School Trustees, Manitoba Association of School Superintendents, Manitoba Association of Parent Councils Inc., and the Manitoba Association of Principals to react to the position papers based on which these bills were developed. Instead of attempting to integrate divergent interests represented by these groups, the government pitched the interests of one group against the other. By the tactics of divide and conquer, the government has poisoned the relationships among these interest groups, notably between, Manitoba Teacher Society and Manitoba Association of School Trustees. The heightened political tension among interest groups do not foster a solid alliance for supporting the implementation of the public policies which have become provincial laws.

Basic Causes for Translating Government Agenda into Public Policies

Given the negative consequences associated with the current process of translating the Manitoba government agenda into public policies, one needs to ask the question as to why it should embark upon such a harmful and potentially disastrous course. The answer to this question should be sought beyond the context of provincial politics. Indeed, the impetus for the present government action originated from both the actions of federal government as well as from the course of actions of other provincial governments. From the historical perspective, there is no lack of evidence that the federal government has shied away from direct intervention in public education in the name of national interests even though it lacks the constitutional jurisdiction to do so (for example, Stevenson, 1981; Sackney, 1990). A more recent action embarked by the federal government in Mulroney's time was the so called "prosperity initiative" (Prosperity Task Force, 1992). Essentially, the federal government was aroused into action in 1991 by the international test competition which placed Canadian students unfavorably in ranks when compared with students from other countries. When the Liberal Party came into power, it continued the established course by assigning a parliamentary committee to examine the national standard and the productivity of science and engineering graduates from Canadian universities (Committee on National Standards in Education, 1994).

This series of federal actions has so shaken the provincial governments across Canada from a state of complacency. To avoid the loss of initiatives in the area that is constitutionally theirs, the once dormant CMEC or the Council of Ministers of Education of Canada (Bergen, 1977) congregated and produced a "Victoria Declaration" which mapped out a Pan-Canadian agenda for revamping Canadian public education from the restructuring of the governance structure, curriculum changes, teacher recertification to all aspects of public education. There is little wonder that when we examine Manitoba "Blue Print" for school reform, it is so similar in content and direction with Nova Scotia's "Education Horizons (Nova Scotia Department of Education, 1995) or Ontario's current agenda. Indeed, there should be little differences in the position papers prepared by all provincial governments, given that they have already reached consensus in the direction and content regarding how changes in the public education should be evolved. These bills that were passed through the Manitoba Legislative Assembly represent only a portion of those that are yet to come.

Within the context of the Western Consortium, where the provincial ministers of education from Manitoba, Saskatchewan, Alberta and British Columbia meet on regular basis, there is further agreement in terms of a time line in getting the public education changes in place. The fear of falling behind the set schedule should explain why there was so little and so hasty public consultation in finalizing the bills in Manitoba.

That the bills examined were predominantly concerned with the financial considerations and centralized control must be intimately related to the declared federal plan of reducing the federal-provincial transfer (Derrin, 1996). Back in 1977, the established program funding (EPS), agreed upon between the federal and provincial governments, specified that the federal government would pay half of the post-secondary and public health expenses. However, the rules governing the EPS were changed in 1982, when the ceiling of federal government contribution was imposed. The annual per-capita EPF transferred amount to provincial governments had been calculated. In 1995, the federal government introduced Canada Health and Social transfer (CHST), Human Resources Investment Fund (HRIF) and employment insurance (EI) to replace the Established Program Funding (Derrin, 1996). With these changes, the federal government aims at reducing the transferred lump sum of $16.6 billion by $2.8 billion in 1996, and further trimming the amount by $1.8 billion in the fiscal year of 1997-8. The federal-provincial transfer will eventually be frozen at $11 billion dollars.

There is little doubt that given all sectors of the public education, health and social services come from the same source, reduction of federal payment in post-secondary education, and two other services will gravely affect funding for the public K-12 school system. With the anticipated transfer decline from the federal government, Manitoba government feels that it has to take full fiscal control of every aspect of the public education (as demonstrated in the contents of all the bills analyzed) to ensure no unexpected out-of-control expenditure has occurred.

What remains not clear from the legislation are the major coping strategies to be adopted by Manitoba Government with the reduction of federal transfer. At present, there are generally three approaches taken by other provincial governments in dealing with the transfer shortfalls. The first is to shield its post-secondary institutions from the effects of the federal cutbacks. This is adopted by the richer provinces like British Columbia. The second is to off-load the full impact onto the post-secondary institutions. This is adopted by the province of Ontario which is shouldered with excessive budget deficits (its annual budget deficit of $8 billion is equivalent to the total accumulated debt of Manitoba). The third is to backfill the federal reduction partially. This is the response strategy of the have-not provinces like Saskatchewan. One could speculate that given Manitoba is not dissimilar in wealth when compared with its Prairie compatriat, it might adopt Saskatchewan's strategy.

Conclusion

The analysis of the public policies adopted by the Manitoba government is most fascinating and rewarding in the sense that these public policies reveal the true intent and purposes of what the provincial government attempts to achieve in the years to come. Equally appealing is the analysis of the process as well as the macro-political factors leading to the formulation and adoption of these policies. The former unearths the current working relationship among various interest groups in the Province. The latter provides a broader scan of what is taking place at the federal-provincial level in Canada. Irrespective of what angle one takes in trying to understand the origins and sources of the public policies, one is convinced that the current approach of school reform is largely governed by the financial concerns at the provincial and federal levels. Governed by the necessity to exercise control over fiscal management comes the natural argument that the power of decision-making should be centralized. The twin- considerations of economization and centralization should provide a proper frame of reference in trying to cope with the new policies adopted by one provincial government or another in the name of restructuring and school reform.

References

Bergen, J.J. (1977). "Council of Minister of Education in Canada: at a political juncture?" In Wallin, J.H.A. (ed.) *The politics of canadian education* (pp. 9-17). 4th Yearbook, Canadian Society for the Study of Education. Edmonton, AB: Western Industrial Research Centre.

Committee on National Standards in Education. (1994). NATIONAL STANDARDS IN EDUCATION: A QUESTION OF EXCELLENCE (Report of the National Advisory Board on Science and Technology). Ottawa: Government of Canada.

Derrin, P. (1996, May). The impact of changes in federal-provincial block transfer. Paper presented at Canadian Education Association Leadership Short Course, Mont. Tremblanc, Quebec.

Downey, L. W. (1988). *Policy analysis in education.* Calgary, AB: Detselig Enterprises Ltd.

Dyck, P.G., Render, S., & Carlyle, J. D. (1995). *Report on the teacher collective bargaining and compensation review committee*. Winnipeg, MB: Government Press.

Guthrie, J.W. *(1977).* "Educational policy research and the pursuit of equality, efficiency and liberty," In Immegart, G.L., & Boyd, W.L. (eds.) *Problem-finding in educational administration* (pp. 87-108). Toronto, ON: D.C. Heath and Co.

Hennessy, P.H. (1977). "Collective bargaining and the professionalization of Ontario teachers," *Teacher Education, 10,* 20-31.

Lam, Y.L.J. (1981). "Collective bargaining: A present and future perspective," *Canadian school executive, 1 (5),* 8-9.

Lam, Y.L.J. & S. L. Kong. (1981). "Effects of collective bargaining on teacher-board relations," *Challenge in Educational Administration, 21 (1),* 25-29.

MacIver, D.(1990). "Policy development in provincial government.," In Lam, Y.L.J. (ed.) *Canadian public education system: issues and prospects* (pp.141-154). Calgary, AB: Detselig Enterprises Ltd.

Manitoba Education and Training (1995). *Renewing education: new directions*. Winnipeg, MB: Government Press.

Manitoba education and training. Winnipeg, MB: School Finance Branch (1991/2).

Manitoba School Divisions/Districts Boundaries Review Commission (1994). *Final report and recommendations*. Winnipeg, MB: Government Press.

National Advisory Board on Science and Technology (1994). *Committee on national standards in education*. Ottawa, ON: Government Press.

Nova Scotia Department of Education (1995). *Education horizons: White paper on restructuring the education system*. Halifax, NS:Government Press.

Ontario School Board Reduction Task Force (1996). *Final report*. Toronto, ON: Government Press.

Prosperity Task Force (1992). *Prosperity through innovation: the task force on challenges in science, technology and related skills, summary report*. Ottawa, ON: Government Press.

Sackney, L.E. (1990). "Federal intrusion in education through immersion and second language programs," In Lam, Y.L.J. (ed.) Canadian public education system: Issues and prospects (pp.121-140). Calgary, AB: Detselig Enterprises Ltd.

Stevenson, H.A. (1981). "The federal presence in Canadian education, 1939-1980." In Ivany J.W.G., & Manley-Casimir, M.E. (eds.) *Federal-provincial relations: education canada* (pp. 3-22). Toronto, ON: OISE Press.

4

Financial Implications to the Decentralization of Public School Systems

Anne L. Jefferson

By and large the public school system has operated on the rationale that its organizational structure will result in the removal of barriers to the learning process. Not only are the barriers removed, the learning process is facilitated. To this end, numerous consultations and debates have engaged the energy of parents, taxpayers, business, and government. The results of these conversations have ranged from a public school system minimally challenged by opposing private systems to expanding challenges within the public system to allow very different structural existences. These structural alternatives have meant a different organizational relationship between the school and the school board. And, at times included different administrative arrangements within the school as well. For the most part, the movements have involved decentralization of the system.

What is surprising is the apparent embrace given to decentralization of the public school system. The acceptance that decentralization needs to be the future of the public school system is evident by a quick browse of the internet. The term decentralization on a given search engine generates hundreds of web sites. Exploration of these sites reveals, however, that the embraces of decentralization have realized unique and shared hurdles and successes. For example, decentralization of the public school system has meant fundamental changes in the way decisions are made and resources allocated. In some circumstances the decisions are shared between the school and the school board. In other cases, the decisions are shared at the school level between the school staff and a parent advisory council. As this governance function is adjusted NCREL (1993) cautions that the decision making parameters must be explicitly understood by all. Otherwise, "well-meaning and dedicated teachers, principals, and parents will become engaged in the task or restructuring, only to find that they have little authority to institute substantive change" (p. 1). The degree to which the decentralization is judged a success is often conditional to the extent this understanding existed.

Another condition that is not consistently evident in decentralized systems is inservicing. Under decentralization, roles of all individuals are refined. Refined roles often mean individuals are expected to have skills that were not demanded previously; for instance, active participation in defining, justifying, and allocating resources. Most educators do not think in terms of the costs of their activities. Instead, they focus on the curriculum and how to apply it to meet the learning needs of their students. Under decentralization the two considerations must be attended to. Unfortunately, without professional development of educators to enable them to understand their curriculum focus in terms of costs, the costs of their activities are not appropriately accounted for and the fail safe of a centralized system is not there to break the fiscal free fall that they have placed their school in.

An explanation for occurrences such as those mentioned above is offered by Rodriguez (1995). He brings to our attention that decentralization will have as its rationale either an administrative and political orientation or a civil orientation. The decentralization of the school system on the basis of an administrative and political orientation or a civil orientation. The decentralization of the school system on the basis of an administrative and political orientation refers to the efficiency of the administration, the distance between those who are being served and those who are providing the service, participation in the system, and the encouragement of all to have a voice in the governance of the schools. The civil orientation, in comparison, refers to individuals with their own behaviors, demands, identities, and committed life styles. This distinction is essential to appreciate. The manner in which these differing orientations interact throughout the decentralization of the system determines the extent to which existing barriers to the learning process are dismantled and removed or are reinforced. Although the former is the objective for participation in decentralization, once the process starts, it is easily overrun by concerns embedded in the uniqueness of both orientations. Thus, good intentions cannot be left unmonitored. The financial implications associated with decentralization supports this stance. These implications will be discussed later in the chapter.

Decentralization of the Public School System

There is no doubt that decentralization is an active choice on how the public school system should be governed. What has not been fully acknowledged is that although at one level decentralization has occurred, at another the status quo may be just as prevalent. As noted by Kazal-Thresher (1993, p. 32),

> ... some of the assumptions regarding the outcomes of school choices may be unwarranted since it is entirely possible that parental choice, per se, would not affect how schools are run. Therefore, school choice, in and of itself, may not speak the kind of reorganization that would lead to technical changes that matter in improving school achievement.

What needs to be clarified is whether the concern and rationale for decentralization is administrative and fiscal or program and structure. Winkler and Rounds (1993) suggests that: "A large number of developing nations are in the process of decentralizing basic education, with the aim of diversifying revenue sources and introduction [of] greater accountability and efficiency." The introduction of charter schools in Canada appear to have a more program and structure justification. This is evident by the guidelines established by the Alberta Ministry of Education (1995). Among the main guidelines are:

> As part of the public education system charter schools must be open to any Alberta student interested in challenging the program provided by the school, as long as space in the school is available. School charters must outline the process to be used to select students when the projected enrolment exceeds the school capacity. Any student or parent who believes that access has been wrongfully denied to a student may appeal to the Minister of Education.
>
> To ensure access is available to any student, charter schools may not charge tuition fees.
>
> The curriculum of a charter school must be structured around the requirement of a basic education as defined by Alberta Education and charter school students must write provincial achievement tests and provincial high school diploma exams.
>
> Charter schools are accountable for their results and for achieving improvements in student learning. A charter school may have its charter revoked by the local school board or Minister of Education should it not follow the requirements of the charter, or if the school is not succeeding.

The intent of the guidelines was underlined by the Minister in his statement, "Providing parents and students with greater choice in curriculum and education delivery methods and improving student learning are the key principles that will guide the establishment and operation of charter schools in the province [Alberta]" (Education Minister Halvar Jonson as quoted in *Alberta Education* News Release, April 21, 1995).

Either the Alberta rationale or the rationale serving developing nations opens up possibilities. The possibilities differing on whether the attempt is to optimize costs or flexibility. The Alberta rationale based more on program and structure is more aligned to a strategy for increasing flexibility by means of user empowerment. The rationale of developing nations, as suggested by Winkler and Rounds (1993), implies an administrative and fiscal orientation. An orientation premised on such a justification is reflexive of a strategy for controlling costs at the same time as allowing a calculated diseconomies of scale.

The strategies, in either instance, are not divorced from such global changes as the advances in technology and the growing professionalism of the work force. As noted by Atkinson (1983), in schools "educational technology tends to increase costs in the expectation of improving learning" (p.131). The latter part of the twentieth century has witnessed an explosion in educational technology. This explosion has raised expectations within and external to the school system to the point that the resources are beyond what a single school system can offer. Partnerships and a restructuring of the system, sometimes by means of decentralization, have been judged as the time approached to adopt for the purpose of securing necessary resources. These resources enable educators to more closely match the learning curve of students with the learning expectations for the students by others.

The growing professionalization of the work force is consistent with many of the values of the professionalism culture, including resistance to bureaucracy (Raelin, 1986). The autonomy sought by the professional educator does not mean the lost of accountability. Instead, accountability in the professional culture is heightened and the push of technology ensures that this culture includes technology. Combined with this is the implication that the learning curve of the educator is enhanced. The result is an enhanced learning curve for the student.

Consequently, there is potential and good reasons to redefine functions between the system and its schools. The above notes what Laine, Greenward, and Hedges (1996) claim is the debate surrounding education reform: "identifying the most educationally effective and efficient allocation of resources, attempting to remove barriers to learning, and creating concordant incentives for students and educators" (p. 44). In doing so, this realignment of functions

> must be effective in the guarantee of a greater governability, in the production of better . . . standards, in the improvement of the public services, in the professionalism of management, . . . Otherwise, it will lose the confidence of the citizenry and will fail . . .(Velasquez 1994, quoted by Rodriquez, 1995)

The Financial Implications of Decentralization

The financial implications of decentralization are often overlooked. Only after the system has committed itself and has moved substantially along the process does fiscal concerns start to emerge. This emergence often causes a reaction and a flurry of actions to somehow develop at least a short term fix.

Yet there is enough understanding of what decentralization means to the public school system that the fiscal concerns could be and should be foci at the start of the process. Some of these concerns are addressed as follows:

• There is the belief that decentralization of the public school system is the solution to the problem of a large bureaucracy and the inefficiency of a centralized institution. Furthermore, it is assumed that this solution guarantees better conditions for the free mobility of the resources. Both given need to be carefully reflected on. Does decentralization represent a greater efficiency in the production and provision of public education? According to the public choice approach, this would occur since individuals and localities would have to assume the economic costs of their decisions. However, decentralization of the public school system has never been taken to mean the loss of established funding or the requirement that individuals and localities would assume additional funding requirements. Consequently, the status quo is taken as a given at least on the fiscal front. This is a false premise. Contrary to the comfort level that these beliefs and assumptions generate, decentralization is labor intensive and thereby causes expenditures to increase.

• Decentralization is conceived as the search of institutional mechanisms that would permit greater participation of the citizenry, and a manner to solve problems close to where they exist. Rodriguez (1995) states:

> It is argued that the concentration and sectorialization of public administration has become expensive, inefficient, bureaucratic and incompetent for incorporating with agility new demands and social and cultural interests. Programs and projects close to the local and daily reality are seen by the society as opportunities for progress that a sectorial oriented central administration denies or blocks.

This rationale is not argued with. However, the lack of knowledge (despite what the citizenry claims) about the learning process and the structural implications can lead to inappropriate demands on the system and ineffective and more costly operational mechanisms. Thus, a considerable amount of resources are needed to educate the citizenry. These resources are generally not new funds but a diversion of funds that would have been allocated to students.

• Decentralization does not ensure a greater equity in attending to a needy population. Campbell (1994, quoted by Rodriguez, 1995) supports this observation noting that "in many occasions that local governments respond more to local necessities, but if these actions are not coordinated with national programs, they are not sustainable in fiscal terms, and, in many senses, they are inherently inequitable and inefficient given current conditions." If equity is to be obtained additional funds in addition to a more centralized as opposed to decentralized approach would have to be present.

• Decentralization of the public school system encourages competition among schools especially if funding is directly related to school enrolment. Thus consideration is given whether enrolling an additional student generates revenues in excess of marginal costs, it can maximize profits by enrolling students up to the school's physical capacity. Elevating the economics of the situation to priority level potentially distracts the school away from the learn needs of students.

• Decentralized schools are obliged to assume the management of services without necessarily having the technical, financial, and political conditions to do so. If these conditions are not present then general frustration will prevail. The locus of power has not followed the restructuring. Once the smoke and mirrors have been cleared what is left is a cracked decentralized mirage. The inseparability of the management of services and the conditions that make those services available have been too often ignored. The limited effects of decentralization attests to this reality.

• Decentralization has produced ambiguous situations as a result of a series of undesired consequences and an unclear plan with previously established objectives (Tenti, 1994, as cited by Rodriguez, 1995). Once again, the costs associated with decisions need to be calculated. The public school system is an established system that is not being eliminated only changed in structure and governance under decentralization. Commitments and obligations are not fiscally free and their fiscal price must be accommodated under decentralization. This bondage is clearly noted in the following quotation:

> The main reason for the limited effects of decentralization is the inseparability of decisions. Linkages among budget, personnel, instructional, and operational decisions mean that "decentralized" authority ostensibly given school staff over one class of decisions has effectively been limited by centralized constraints on other classes of decisions. For example, a school might have discretion over the selection of supplementary textbooks, but this decision is dependent on how much money is available for educational materials, and discretion over that decision resides with the parent school district.

Conclusion

Decentralization attempts to respond to diversity, to find diverse answers to the problems of heterogenous territories and social groups. The option for decentralization implies recognition and acceptance of differences and the formulation of programs for dissimilar realities in order to arrive at similar results.

In attempting to achieve this objective, it must be remembered that the public school system is an expense driven institution and decentralization will mean an even closer examination of the process and its outcomes relative to the inputs. The extent to which the public school system is responsive to the ebbs and flows of the economy will be a measuring stick. Yet, the needs of the students have multiplied. This multiplication is made more complex as the cultural diversity of students grow with increasing speed. The right program for the individual student is the demand for the dollars allocated. In a decentralized system who defines "the right program" is not always clear.

The quality indicators that will be accepted and subsequently determine what funding will be made available could conceivably be narrowly defined and reflect the needs and demands of a small sector of society. The result would be a shrinking of the student choice with respect to what role to assume upon graduation. Should this happen, a decentralized school system serves an externally identified need as opposed to the student needs. Only with a deliberate change in mindset that accounts for the costs of the learning organization, the public school, by those charged with the responsibility of the decentralized system will the needs of all students remain the priority.

References

Alberta Education. (1995, April 21). News release. Edmonton.

Atkinson, G.B.J. (1983). *The economics of education.* Toronto: Hodder and Stoughton.

Author unknown. (1996, January 22). The trade-offs of decentralization. Internet: http://www.ndma.com/hotc/bprka.htm.

Hess, M. (1996, February 15). IS reorganization: Centralization vs. decentralization. Internet; http://www.gartner.com/hotc/bprka.htm.

Kazal-Threshner, D.M. (1993). "Educational expenditures and school achievement: When and how money can make a difference," *Educational Researcher,* March, 30-32

Laine, R., Greenward, R. & Hedges, L.V. (1996). "Money does matter: A research of a new universe of education production function studies." In L.O. Picus and J.L. Wattenbarger (eds.). *Where does the money go? Resource allocation in elementary and secondary schools* (pp.44-70). Thousand Oaks, CA: Corwin Press.

NCREL (1993). Decentralization: Why, how and toward what ends? Internet: http://www.ncrel.org./ncrel/sdrs/areas/issues/envrnmnt/go/93-lcomm.htm.

Raelin J.A. (1986). *The clash of cultures.* Boston: Harvard Business School Press.

RAND. (1995). The decentralization mirage. Internet: http.//www.rand.org/publications/RRR/RRR.winter94.5.education/Decentralization.html.

Rodriguez, A. (1995). The contents of decentralization: Concept, objectives, pros and cons, and challenges. Internet: http://www.idrc.ca/socdev/document.

Winkler, D.R., & Rounds, T. (1993). Municipal and private sector response to decentralization and school choice: The case of Chile, 1981-1990. A paper prepared for the International Symposium on Economics of Education, Manchester, England, May 1993.

5

Financing Aboriginal Education

K.P. Binda

Jurisdiction and Fiduciary Responsibility

In preliterate traditional societies the responsibility for enculturating and educating their young children into the folkways, mores, culture and skills, necessary for successful living, rested primarily with the family, kinship group and band members. The patterned way of thinking, feeling and behaving that the young acquired, consciously or unconsciously, resulted from direct or indirect teachings from the elders who saw that the younger generation adopted the traditional ways of thinking and behaving. Failure to adopt the group's culture, quite naturally meant disruption in the continuity of things and the possible demise of the group, since culture is the primary mode of achieving reproductive success (Harris, 1975). The process of enculturation ensured the continuity of the life-ways from one generation to the next and it was supported, controlled and managed by the community in situ.

However, in Canada the nature of this cross-generational continuity among the First Nations slowly eroded over the last two hundred years with the coming of the Europeans, particularly the missionaries, obsessed with civilizing, christianizing, proselytizing and colonizing.

First Nations in this context are those aboriginal inhabitants of Canada who fall under the jurisdiction of the various Indian Acts and Treaties and whose welfare, particularly education, is a direct responsibility of the Federal Government. The Inuit are the aboriginal inhabitants residing primarily in the Arctic regions and who were previously called Eskimos. Like the First Nations with treaty rights, the Federal Government, through the Territorial governments, funds the education of the Inuit including those residing in Quebec and Labrador. The Métis, who are often referred as aboriginal peoples, are primarily under the jurisdiction of provincial authorities who have responsibility for their education.

With the founding of the Canadian state in 1867, control and responsibility for educating aboriginal children shifted from the First Nations' communities to the state, with the churches playing proxy roles for the assimilation process. Section 91 (23) of the *British North America Act, 1867* (now the Constitution Act, 1867) gave the Federal Government jurisdiction over Indians and lands reserved for Indians. Subsequent treaties with the First Nations and Acts of Parliament such as the Indian Acts of 1868, 1876, 1951 and 1985, further enshrined the fiduciary responsibility of the Federal Government for educating First Nations.

After the patriation of the Canadian constitution in 1982 the BNA Act was renamed the *Constitution Act, 1982*. Section 25 of this act forms part of the new Charter of Rights and Freedoms and includes an affirmation of existing treaty and land claim agreements. Section 35 (1) of the Constitution Act 1982 further affirmed that "the existing aboriginal and treaty rights of the aboriginal peoples of Canada are hereby recognized and affirmed." In the Act "aboriginal peoples of Canada" include Indian, Inuit and Métis. As noted above, education of the Métis is covered by the provincial authorities, the Métis having no treaties guaranteeing them education rights such as those for the (Indians) First Nations.

Specific responsibilities for the education of First Nations are outlined in detail in Sections 114 to 123 of the Indian Act. These sections empower the Federal Minister of Indian and Northern Affairs (DIAND now INAC) to carry out the responsibilities which include curriculum, instruction agreements with various authorities and a wide range of educational and student support services for First Nations from pre-kindergarten to post-secondary programs. Kindergarten programs were authorized by Treasury Board in 1958. The Department is also authorized to fund cultural/educational centres, and First Nations political associations' education offices. All funding of education related activities are authorized under Treasury Board arrangements and the Financial Administration Act of Parliament. The ultimate source of Canada's legal commitment for First Nations' education itself rests in the treaties with First Nations from which the various acts of Parliament emanate. This fiduciary commitment to First Nations has been consistently reinforced across Canada in recent years by both the Federal Government and First Nations. In a *Memorandum of Understanding 1994,* between the Minister of INAC on behalf of Canada, and the Grand Chief on behalf of the Assembly of Manitoba Chiefs (AMC), as well as in the dismantling *Framework Agreement* (1994), and *Education Framework Agreement* (1990) in Manitoba, the funding guarantee was reaffirmed (INAC-AMC, 1994; 1990).

The Government of Canada White Paper of 1969 (Chrétien, 1969) which developed from recommendations made by the Hawthorn Report of 1967, (Hawthorn, 1967) another commission on First Nations, proposed the elimination of all constitutional and legislative bases of discrimination in favor of Indians. The proposal generated a political firestorm (Binda, 1996) locally and nationally among the First Nations communities. First Nations responded with their own paper, *Indian Control of Indian Education* (NIB 1972). The government backed away and, on June 23, 1972, the Honorable Jean Chrétien, Minister of DIAND, in a speech at Regina to the Council of Ministers of Education, announced the Federal Government's legal responsibility for educating First Nations children. Chrétien accepted *Indian Control of Indian Education* and further stated his government's new policy of transferring jurisdiction with the financial supports directly to the First Nations Bands. In addition, he outlined the conditions that impacted First Nations education and the obligations which provincial education authorities should take or consider in the education of First Nations children in their jurisdictions. Some of these concerns were: the importance of curriculum, teachers, administration, parental participation, social and cultural relevance, quality of instruction and community input (Chrétien, 1972). This new initiative represented a watershed in federal policy development, not only in jurisdiction, but also concomitantly, in financing First Nations education. This policy marked the true beginning of the First Nations movement for self-government, and education was the first sphere for the government's sectorial approach to devolution for First Nations.

That education was the first area of activity targeted for devolution was not surprising. Education and its attendant funding arrangements was perhaps the best or most developed area of delivery service to First Nations that the Federal Government provided. Education was the primary service sector that the Federal Government utilized, with the churches as proxy agents, for the assimilation of aboriginal children into the wider Canadian society. The church-run residential schools have been severely criticized for the abhorrent practices they inflicted upon the helpless aboriginal children, and their dysfunctional effects are believed to be the root causes of many of the problems facing First Nations today. The residential schools were funded by the Federal Government as part of its fiduciary responsibility to First Nations. These schools were phased out in the 1970s as the policy of local control was increasingly implemented or, as more and more First Nations students attended Federal schools that replaced the residential schools, or provincial schools through direct funding of tuition agreements.

Funding and Management Framework Issues

It is generally accepted that the Federal Government has fiduciary responsibility for educating First Nations covered by treaties. However, the management, funding and delivery of programs to First Nations students have been problematic. A report by DIAND (1982) pointed out that

> no effective national or regional structures have been developed to establish the character of Indian education as distinctive, complex, yet forming a recognizable whole within Canadian education. (p. 41)

The report further noted that at

> no time has the Federal Government developed the institutional framework to enable it to deliver comprehensive educational services to Indians. (p.40)

The report also noted that prior to 1973, Departmental education policy inhibited the development of appropriate structure and delivery mechanisms for a contemporary education system. Figure 1 illustrates deficiencies in DIAND's delivery system when compared with the education systems of provinces at that time.

B.C.	ALBERTA	DIAND
SCHOOLS (A.D.M.)		
PUBLIC INSTRUCTION		

Basic Programs
  Curriculum Development
  Learning Assessment
  Career Programs
  French Language Services
  Examinations
	Curriculum A.V. Services
	  Language, Science etc.
	  Consultants
	
	Language Services: Translation
	Student evaluation & data processing
	Early Childhood: Field Consultants
		Reduced curriculum development funding
		Consultant positions reduced
		
		No systematic student evaluation

Special Education
  Special Education
  Indian Education
  Handicapped
	Special Education: Guidance
	  & counselling
	Industrial education
		Little special education
		Guidance Counsellor positions reduced

Program Implementation	Field services: Regional Offices	Supervision reduced
LEGISLATIVE SERVICES		
Print Services Media Centre	School Book Branch A.V. Library Program	No centralized curriculum material or audio-visual services
ADMINISTRATIVE SERVICES		

Correspondence Courses
Publications
	Support Division
	  Student evaluation
	  Alberta Correspondence Schools
	  School Book Branch
		No services

EDUCATIONAL PERSONNEL		
Educational Personnel Teacher Services Accreditation and School Evaluation	Personnel Services	No services within education Limited school evaluation - lack PY's
POST-SECONDARY (A.D.M.)		
CONTINUING EDUCATION	(	
Continuing Education Adult Basic	(((	University and Professional Program supported Adult Basic almost entirely eliminated for budgetary reasons
MANAGEMENT SERVICES	(	

Planning and Analysis
  Training Projects
  Manpower Training
  Student Services
	(SEPARATE
	(
	(
	(MINISTRY
		Student services reduced

PROGRAM SERVICES	(	
College Programs Research and Development	((	Funding of external agencies only - no developmental work possible
MINISTRY SERVICES (A.D.M.)		
POLICY DEVELOPMENT	Policy Analysis & Development Issue-oriented research	Little capacity No research capability
PERSONNEL SERVICES	Personnel	No services under Education
DATA & INFORMATION		

Data Services
  Project Planning
  Information Services
 	
  Library
	Student evaluation & data processing
	Planning & Research: consultants
	Communications: Public Relations
	Educational Communications & Technology
	Library Services
		Nominal roll information only
		No positions in Education
		NIL
		
		No circulation to schools

FINANCIAL SERVICES		
Schools Finance Post Secondary Finance Ministry Finance	Finance, Statistics & Legislation Legal Advisor Internal Auditor Records	Services external to Education
FACILITIES SERVICES		
Schools Facilities Post-Secondary Facilities	School Building Administration	Construction and maintenance not controlled by Education

Source: DIAND 1982

Figure 1: Education System Elements

As shown in Figure 1, provincial education systems are very much integrated and complete, with sub-parts of each system interacting with other sectors within the larger provincial system to perform the necessary functions of planning, budgeting and program implementation in a coherent and efficient manner. The reduced and perhaps inefficient capabilities of the federal department in the area of Aboriginal education may have been in the very organization and management structure. In fact, the paper by DIAND (1982) cited before, pointed out that "the problem is rooted in a variety of other organizational and environmental factors." (p.23). For example, within DIAND, two headquarters education units *operations* and *development* had separate responsibilities for education, violating an important theoretical principal of unity of command. It was not unusual for one unit not to know what the other was doing. This condition did not exist within provincial systems; it has been a major factor in the call for the development of a more efficient system as proposed by First Nations through devolution, for example, the *Education Framework Agreement* in Manitoba (AMC, 1995) and the Mi'Kmaq Education Agreement 1997, in Nova Scotia (Irwin, 1997). The new proposed structures are dealt with in more detail further in this chapter.

A poorly defined management system quite naturally impacted upon funding and resource allocation. This in turn impacted upon the quality of education. Historically aboriginal children, as a cohort in Canada, have had the lowest educational achievement, highest age-grade retardation, highest dropout and withdrawal rates and low participation rates in the economic fabric of this country including depressed income earning capacity. (AMC, 1991; AFN, 1988; Battiste and Barman, 1995; Binda, 1995; 1996; 1997; Burns, 1996; Common and Frost, 1994; MacPherson, 1991; Ministry of Colleges and Universities, 1991; Royal Commission on Aboriginal Peoples [RCAP], 1996; York, 1992.) Not only in educational achievements, but in every sphere of activity, the position of aboriginal peoples when compared with other Canadians is nothing short of scandalous. Aboriginal conditions have been extensively documented in numerous reports, commissions and studies, the most recent of which is the *Royal Commission on Aboriginal Peoples* (1996) and need not be further elaborated on.

A good measure of the problem can be traced back, as stated earlier, to the organization, management and funding structures for aboriginal education. The

DIAND study (1982) reported that " a common theme in all the analysis of the issues is that a funding problem exists in most areas of the education program." (p. 43). The study further noted that "funding issues have loomed large in the Department's dialogue on education with Indian people," and that "no clearly identifiable guiding principle concerning the funding of Indian education has been discernable to this point in time." (p. 43). In another study (Assembly of Manitoba Chiefs, 1991) which was spearheaded by a former Deputy Minister of Education in Manitoba, the investigation concluded that,

> the educational problems of Indian communities in Manitoba are severe and deeply rooted. They cannot be solved with ordinary levels of financial support, because the usual Canadian standards of educational services are inadequate to the needs of Indian communities. New approaches to education funding as well as additional resources are badly needed. (p.ii)

This study further noted,

> the present INAC formula was introduced without consultation with Indian people. There is little evidence that the basic elements in the formula are educationally appropriate. Many elements critical to a quality education program are not covered by the current formula. (p.i)

The AMC study pointed out that the current formula (described further on) used to disburse funds supported levels of expenditure that varied widely from community to community within both federal and band-operated schools (and within tuition agreements as well). For example, within two federal schools in Northern Manitoba, there was a 179 percent difference in pupil expenditures on instruction – $8 420. per pupil in one school, as against $3 017. in the other school. A 68 percent difference was observed in band-operated schools in the province. The study tried to explain the wide variations by examining all possible factors and concluded that the variations could "not be explained educationally" (AMC, 1991, p. 16).

Given the fact that education related expenditures of DIAND (now renamed INAC: Indian and Northern Affairs Canada) constitute the largest

1981-1982	Total Inschool Expenditures for Elementary/Secondary Education	$255.3 million
	Post-secondary (1985-1986)	$73.7 million
1987-1989	Total DIAND Budget	$4.3 million
	Elementary/Secondary Education	$899 million
	Post Secondary Education	$275 million
	Schools, Infrastructure & Housing	$983 million

Sources: DIAND, 1982; INAC, 1997a

Figure 2: DIAND Education Programs' Cost for the Fiscal Years 1981-82

individual program expense incurred by DIAND, the above observations about management issues become alarming from three important funding issues: efficiency, equity and quality. In fact *Tradition and Education* (AFN, 1988), notes that funding by the Federal Government "do not meet the requirements of First Nations communities and are inadequate to meet the treaty obligations" (p. 42). This point was reiterated in the AMC study (1991) mentioned before. This study concluded that current approaches to funding was "deeply flawed and ought to be replaced" (p. 17). Figure 2 shows expenditures for education for the years 1981/82 and 1997/98. The increase observed in the latter year results from increased enrolment (Fig. 3a), increased retention rates (Fig. 3b), as well as increased numbers attending post-secondary institutions (Fig. 3c).

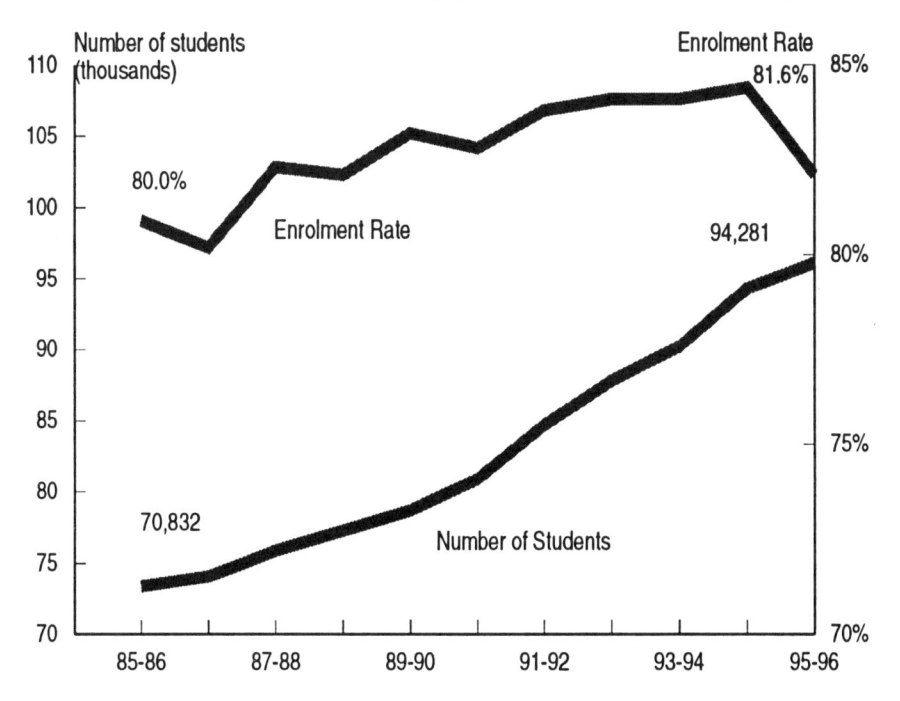

Source: INAC. 1996.

Figure 3a: Elementary/Secondary Enrolment on Reserves (registered Indians 4-18 years)

Other flaws in the funding arrangements have been noted by intervenors in the *Royal Commission on Aboriginal Peoples* (Cassidy, 1992). The intervenors felt that DIAND promoted migration off reserves as a means of reducing the federal fiduciary responsibility for aboriginal people. Under Section 4(3) of the Indian Act (1985), elementary/secondary programs and services are provided for residents on reserves or on Crown lands. This is referred to as the eligibility criteria. Phil Fontaine, formerly Grand Chief of the Assembly of Manitoba Chiefs at the time he gave evidence, and now National Grand Chief of the Assembly of First nations, said "that the rights that we have or that we

Percent

Year	Percent
85-86	33.9
87-88	40.2
89-90	41.6
91-92	53.6
93-94	77.7
95-96	75.1

Source: INAC. 1996.

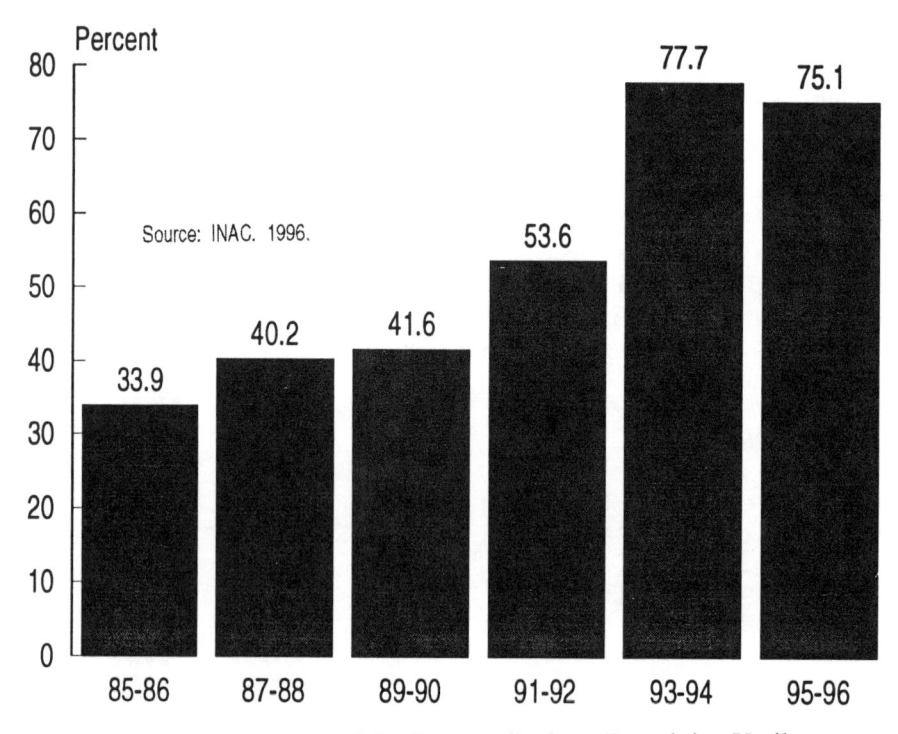

Figure 3b: Percentage of On-Reserve Students Remaining Until Grade 12

Number of Students: 11,170 (85-86) → 26,305 (95-96)
Expenditures: $74M (85-86) → $260M (95-96)

Source: INAC. 1996.

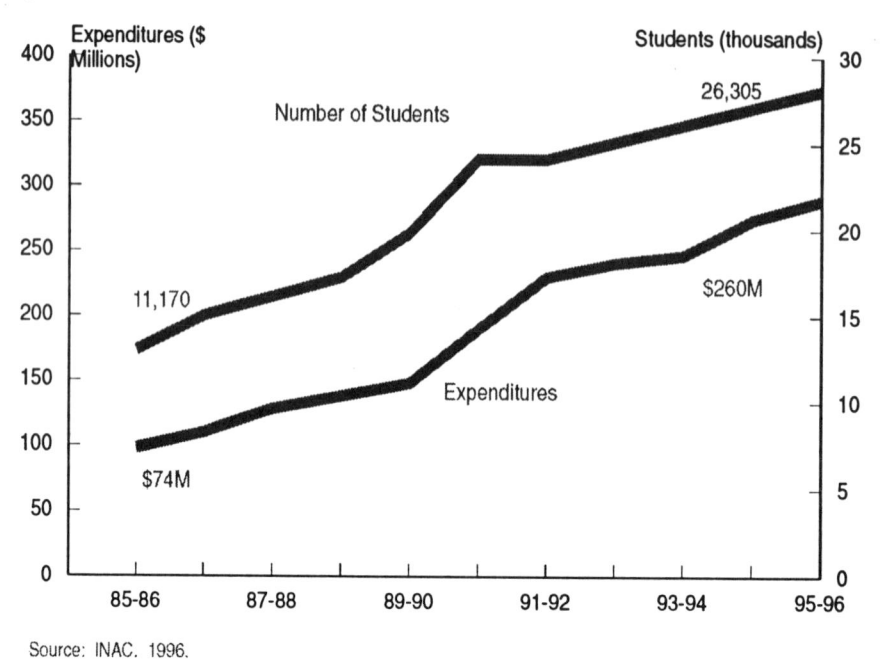

Figure 3c: PSE Enrolment and Expenditures

are supposed to enjoy as beneficiaries of Treaty Agreements that our ancestors signed are portable." (Cassidy, 1992, p.21). When Aboriginal people migrate to urban centres, the Federal Government argues that they are like any immigrant coming to Canada, and as such, fall under provincial jurisdiction. Ontario, through its *Education Act,* R.S.O., 1980, C 129, as amended, accepts this interpretation. Some school divisions across the country, for example, Mystery Lake School Division in Thompson, and Winnipeg School Division No. 1 in Manitoba and others, like the Calgary Public School Board, similarly treat First Nations students in their communities like any other resident in the province.

The provinces argue that they are still a federal responsibility, a claim supported by the First Nations themselves. This argument is advanced by the provinces, particularly when they are called upon to fund special programs that are additional to normal tuition fees. This tug-of-war over fiduciary responsibility has had negative effects on aboriginal people as provincial and federal governments argue about which education system aboriginal people belong to and who is responsible for their funding. Perhaps with devolution and new approaches to funding, such as Alternative Funding Arrangements (AFA), these problems may be resolved or even eradicated altogether. In the meantime, variations in the various systems continue to exist.

Operational Systems and Education Management Regíme

The education program of INAC consists of two main systems: Elementary/Secondary Education and Post-Secondary Education. In addition, funding is also available for other education activities such as Cultural Education Centres. Capital and infrastructures for education are accounted in the INAC budget-planning process but included as a separate category. INAC's policy is to provide

> funding to ensure access to elementary and secondary education for status Indians and Inuit children living on reserve or on Crown lands. These education programs should both be comparable in quality to those provided by the provinces and relevant to First Nations and Inuit students. ... It provides funds to First Nations authorities to ensure that educational programs and services meet the needs of both the students and their communities. (INAC, 1996a, p. 25)

DIAND's support for education stems from its fiduciary responsibility, already discussed, and from the recognition that education is a key factor in reducing welfare dependency, increasing job prospects and in achieving self-sufficiency to the benefit of not only Aboriginal people but the nation as a whole. Recent developments in Aboriginal education point to the increasing efficacy of the latter utilitarian principles. Recent devolution developments also show drastic changes in the structure of the education management regíme. As shown in Figure 4, the proportion of children enrolled in band-controlled schools has been increasing and, inversely, the proportion in federal schools has been declining. Provincial schools also have seen declines in their intake of status aboriginal children, through the continuing relatively large cohort in these schools mainly represents students funded under tuition agreements, where secondary education is not available on reserves. In 1976/77 there were 64 band-operated schools. This number increased to 425 in 1995/96, accounting for over 57 percent of all status children. According to 1995/96 INAC data, provincial schools enrolled about 42 percent of status children while federal schools accounted for less than 2 percent.

School Year	Federal	Provincial	Band-operated	Private	Total
1976/77	30,012	36,884	3,340	1,481	71,717
1977/78	29,412	41,358	5,639	1,679	78,088
1978/79	28,605	45,438	5,796	1,520	81,359
1979/80	27,742	45,742	6,311	1,442	81,237
1980/81	26,578	46,852	7,879	1,492	82,801
1981/82	22,525	43,652	13,133	1,156	80,466
1982/83	21,825	38,511	15,912	1,164	77,412
1983/84	21,893	39,474	16,715	---	78,082
1984/85	21,669	40,080	18,372	---	80,121
1985/86	19,943	39,712	20,968	---	80,623
1986/87	18,811	40,053	23,407	---	82,271
1987/88	17,322	40,520	26,429	---	84,271
1988/89	13,783	40,954	30,845	---	85,582
1989/90	11,764	41,720	34,674	---	88,158
1990/91	8,052	43,453	40,513	---	92,018
1991/92	6,180	43,092	45,665	1,657	96,594
1992/93	5,096	44,418	49,426	1,950	100,890
1993/94	3,453	44,331	53,312	2,548	103,644
1994/95	2,219	44,118	58,139	2,615	107,091
1995/96	1,794	43,787	62,527	2,534	110,642[1]

Note

1. Excludes an estimated 473 students enrolled in band schools from the Nuu-Chah-Nulth Tribal Council, which has negotiated a separate agreement with DIAND. Between 1983/94 and 1990/91, private school data were not coded separately and were collapsed into provincial school figures.

Source: Basic Departmental Data 1996, DIAND.

Figure 4: Total Kindergarten, Elementary and Secondary Renrolment by School Type, On-Reserve Population, Canada 1976-77

The shift in enrolment in the education management regíme is congruent with the devolution movement taking place between the federal government and First Nations communities. This means that funds for educating status children increasingly are being channelled to the bands. Since the federal government no longer negotiates tuition agreements, having withdrawn from this area of activity with the repeal of the Master Tuition Agreement (MTA) between Ottawa and the provinces in June 1992, funding through Tuition Agreements goes directly to the bands or tribal councils who then negotiate with the relevant authorities. Similarly, post-secondary funding is mainly administered by First Nations as more than 90 percent of these funds go to students through the bands or tribal authorities. For all categories of students, INAC has laid out specific conditions for the provision of funds. The conditions have been a constant source of irritation for First Nations.

Funding for *elementary/secondary students* is based on the Nominal Roll, a computerized historical data base containing information on all eligible First Nations children. The Nominal Roll is a student census as at September 30 of the academic year. It is utilized to access funding for band-operated and provincial schools, private home placement, transportation and space accommodation calculation. In 1997 the deadline date for submission to INAC was October 15. The submission to INAC must be accompanied by certification as to correctness and eligibility (INAC, 1997b). A special form called the *Nominal Roll Census* form requires the following information: student identification, registration numbers, full name, date of birth, status code, details of residence, accommodation, band of financial responsibility, transportation arrangements, special education needs and language of entry and instruction (INAC 1995). Additionally, all band schools must submit, by October 30 (for 1997), an *Annual Program Certification* for the current year verifying that

> all classroom teachers and the principal possess teaching certificates which are current and valid in the province and that the curriculum being used in the school in all grades meets basic provincial requirements, and lists of each teacher's degree and educational institution. (INAC 1997c).

The allocation for the band-administered schools is based upon a formula and the nominal roll and includes the six factors identified in Figure 5. Resourcing by the formula includes costs for the areas identified in Figure 6. The funding policy for 1997 attempts to take into consideration some of the criticisms directed at the way in which the formula was developed previously. Some of these criticisms have already been mentioned.

Funding for students in provincial or private schools is facilitated through tuition agreements with provinces, school boards or private schools. With devolution taking place now and the withdrawal of INAC from tuition agreements, bands or tribal councils generally make arrangements with individual agencies. Whatever the arrangement, the program must meet INAC "policies, standards, requirements and controls" and "must carry the endorsement of the recipients and the Minister" of INAC (INAC, 1997c. p. 6). The provincial tuition program is made up of regular tuition, special education and language development. The provincial tuition budget is calculated using the number of students and tuition rates provided by the appropriate school authority or division.

Factors
- a) units
- b) student base allocation
- c) special education
- d) adjustment factor
- e) administrative system allocation
- f) red circled special education

Units
Nominal Roll - September 1996

Student Base Allocation
- base - $4,140.00
- amount established in relationship to the regional allocation
- this is for all services in the band administered school

Special Education
- amount - $581.00
- includes gifted, talented, resource and Level I

Adjustment Factors
- two factors utilized:

  a) 1/2 of band remoteness index   b) school size adjustment

» if number of students per grade is less than or equal to 3	0.875
» if number of students per grade is greater than 3 and less than or equal to 6	0.575
» if number of students per grade is greater than 6 and less than or equal to 8	0.275
» if number of students per grade is greater than 8 and less than or equal to 11	0.100
» if number of students per grade is greater than 11	0.000

Administrative System Allocation/Small School
- this is factored as follows:

0 - 50 students	$ 5,000.00
51 - 100 students	10,000.00
101 - 150 students	15,000.00
151+ students	20,000.00

Formula Calculation
[Units X (student base allocation + special education) x adjustment factor] = administration systems allocation + special education red circled.

Source: INAC (1997). Education Management Regime.

Figure 5: Band-Administered School Formula 1997-98

Tuition agreements have come a long way since their inception in the 1950s and 1960s. Previously the Master Tuition Agreements were bilateral agreements between DIAND and provincial school boards. Indian bands were generally excluded from these agreements. This policy created a great deal of friction and bitterness between INAC, school boards and First Nations who claimed that school boards ignored their concerns and were only interested in the funding (Ontario Minister of Education and Training, 1993). Since the withdrawal of the federal government from this sphere of activity, Indian bands have been more aggressive in demanding representation or local school boards as well as more value for money. In Ontario, representation on local school boards is mandated where there are at least 100 native students. In other jurisdictions, for example, Powell River, British Columbia, the local band and school board negotiate a type of agreement that is mutually acceptable to both parties as well as with INAC according to INAC's established policies for funding.

Formula allocation includes:

a) teacher salaries and E.I. benefits
b) paraprofessional salaries and E.I. benefits
c) administration support
   - in the school
d) professional development
e) education leave
f) cultural education
g) native language
h) substitute teachers
i) travel and removal of staff
j) instructional supplies
k) student supplies
l) instructional equipment
   - not capital
m) curriculum development
n) Level I special education including gifted, remedial, clinical services and resource
o) advice and assistance
   - Director of Education and staff
p) board costs
q) salary adjustments

Formula allocation excludes:

a) maintenance and operation
b) transportation of pupils
c) guidance and counselling
d) facility rental
e) Level II and III special education
f) Band Support/Tribal Council Funding
g) Band Employees Benefits
h) minor capital/major capital
i) Education Program evaluations
j) post-secondary
k) private home placement

Source: INAC (1997). Education Management Regime.

Figure 6: Formula Allocation 1997-98

Funding for post-secondary education has been at the discretion of INAC, but insisted upon by First Nations as part of their treaty rights. INAC has argued that post-secondary education was not covered by treaties. Nevertheless, INAC provides funding to the bands that have students in post-secondary institutions. INAC's policy is to insist that funding "allocation will be subject to parliamentary appropriations" (INAC, 1977b), a move perhaps to dampen the growing need for more funds. Post-secondary student enrolment increased from 11 170 in 1985-86 to 26,305 in 1995-96 (INAC, 1996b). Like elementary/secondary funding, strict guidelines are insisted upon by INAC. Any deficit in this area, INAC cautions, is the "responsibility of the recipient." Funding is allocated to the bands on the basis of the previous year funding, plus any increases that Parliament approves. The increase for 1997-98 fiscal year was 1.1 percent.

The guideline for funding is the *Post-Secondary Student Registry* a census similar to the Nominal Roll. All registered students must attend INAC approved institutions and the numbers enrolled are sent to INAC by November 1st. On-site data quality review for verification are performed in May, June and July by INAC. INAC further notes that "in addition to the reporting requirements of the student registry, graduate data must be reported" (INAC, 1997b) on the approved form by November 30th.

In addition to INAC's funding, the provinces through their education departments provide education services to First Nations to the extent of millions of dollars. Curriculum resources and other technical services are provided by department consultants. In Ontario for example, for the fiscal year 1993-94 about $6 million in grants were made available to post-secondary institutions, colleges and universities to improve programs and services for aboriginal people. Under the Aboriginal Education and Training Strategy four funding envelopes were made available, "each designed to address a specific range of needs and to meet the goals of the strategy" (Ontario MET, 1994, p. 2). The four envelopes are: the Support Services Fund, Support Services Enhancement Fund, Program Development Component Fund and, Supplementary Grant Fund. All these programs are reflective of the increasing mobility of the aboriginal population and their roles in the economic development of the country.

Annual financial audits are required for all education programs. As INAC gradually withdraws from direct involvement with First Nations education, through its policy of devolution, it has encouraged First nations to be responsible to their people (Schnitzer, 1990) and develop generally accepted accounting principles and auditing standard as defined by the Canadian Institute of Chartered Accountants. Scott Serson, the Deputy Minister of INAC, speaking to the Public Accounts Committee of Parliament on December 10, 1996, stated that "accountability and value for money must be assured at all levels." He told the Committee that "the department has also strengthened its monitoring of First Nations" programs and that the "majority of First Nations are handling their finances effectively." Serson (1996) further noted that as First nations move towards self-government they "must have flexibility and authority to address the needs of their communities."

Alternative Funding Arrangements and Devolution

In his report to the Public Accounts Committee of the House of Commons in 1996, Serson noted that "Self-government is the cornerstone of our relationship with aboriginal peoples and we are making great strides toward that goal." He further noted that twenty years ago most services were delivered to First nations by federal civil servants "who taught school" as well. Most of "these programs and services" noted Serson, "are delivered by Aboriginal governments. As noted previously, the shift in policy towards Aboriginal control was announced by Chretién in 1972. In Manitoba by 1995, for example, all the bands have control and are delivering their own education services to their people. Other bands across the country are doing likewise. In February, 1997, an agreement lasting the next 5 years with the Mi'Kmaq of Nova Scotia provided approximately $140 million of funding for all education services on and off the reserve. In his address the Minister (Irwin, 1997) pointed out that the "funding will also provide for the operation and maintenance of facilities, band administration and capital." The minister further commented that with the agreement "jurisdiction is returned where it should be, with the Mi'Kmaq people." The process of devolution in education and the accompanying funding has advanced its greatest in Manitoba where on December 10, 1990 the Minister of INAC signed an *Education Framework Agreement* (EFA) with the Assembly of Manitoba Chiefs. The main goal of this agreement is the return of control over education to the First Nations of Manitoba. In December, 1994 a *Framework Agreement* signed between the Minister of INAC and the AMC hoped to totally dismantle INAC in Manitoba and turn over all its activities directly to the AMC.

Prior to the EFA, INAC had explored various formats for giving more responsibility to First Nations who complained bitterly that devolution merely meant *delegated authority* without true control. Such complaints were heard again and again in *Tradition and Education* (AFN 1988). INAC began exploring with Alternative Funding Arrangements (AFA) in 1986. AFA represents a policy change by INAC and intended to provide First Nations with more authority to control their affairs at the community level. The AFA is a signed funding agreement between bands or tribal councils and the Government of Canada for delivering programs to First Nations. The new relationship gives bands/tribal councils the authority and flexibility to manage programs as well as the freedom to move funds between programs without hindrance from INAC officials. In Manitoba the first AFA was signed in 1988 (Salasan, 1991). All First Nations Bands in Manitoba have moved to this new funding arrangement. Under AFA's accountability is maintained with rigid procedures audit as shown in Figure 7.

Since the Education Framework Agreement was signed in Manitoba in 1990, the Assembly of Manitoba Chiefs has been working on the process of devolution and developed a two-tier model. Under the model bands will be involved in the new Manitoba First Nations Education Board while retaining control for their communities. The model (Figure 8) proposes governance and administration with a budget equal to 2 percent of the annual expenditures of INAC for First Nations education in Manitoba.

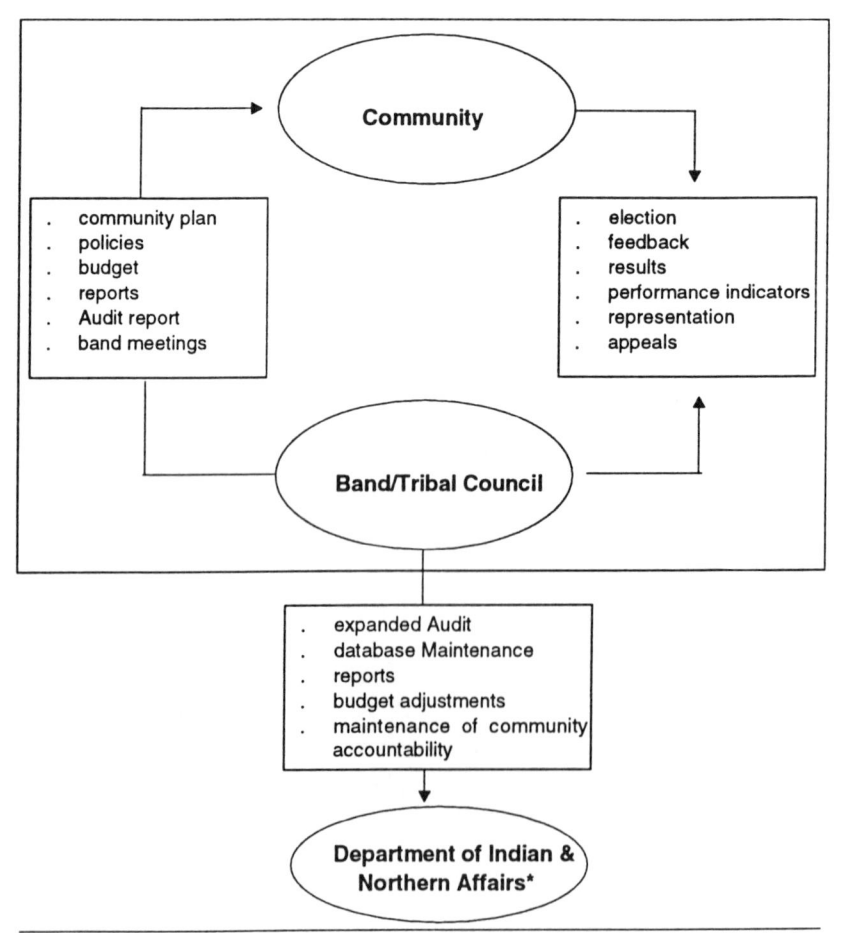

```
                        ┌──────────────┐
                        │  Community   │
                        └──────────────┘
   ┌──────────────────┐                  ┌──────────────────────┐
   │ . community plan │                  │ . election           │
   │ . policies       │                  │ . feedback           │
   │ . budget         │                  │ . results            │
   │ . reports        │                  │ . performance indicators │
   │ . Audit report   │                  │ . representation     │
   │ . band meetings  │                  │ . appeals            │
   └──────────────────┘                  └──────────────────────┘
                        ┌────────────────────┐
                        │ Band/Tribal Council│
                        └────────────────────┘
                                 │
                        ┌───────────────────────────┐
                        │ . expanded Audit          │
                        │ . database Maintenance    │
                        │ . reports                 │
                        │ . budget adjustments      │
                        │ . maintenance of community│
                        │   accountability          │
                        └───────────────────────────┘
                                 │
                        ┌──────────────────────┐
                        │ Department of Indian &│
                        │  Northern Affairs*   │
                        └──────────────────────┘
```

* INAC relationship to First Nations: (a) responsibility under Indian Act/Treaties to First Nation communities; (b) delegation of authority and responsibility to Band/Tribal Council.

Source: Salasan Associates (1991). Research Report: Alternative Funding Arrangements. Winnipeg: Salasan.

Figure 7: Outline of the Band/Tribal Council AFA Accountability Framework

Some First Nations have expressed concern that control will shift from the community to a provincial level. Such fears are reflective of their experiences with INAC. The developments in Manitoba were to have been in place by 1996 but have been delayed to give bands more time to discuss the transfer.

GOVERNANCE

```
Communities
    |
Main Board
Elders & ex-officio members
    |
Executive Board
```

ADMINISTRATION

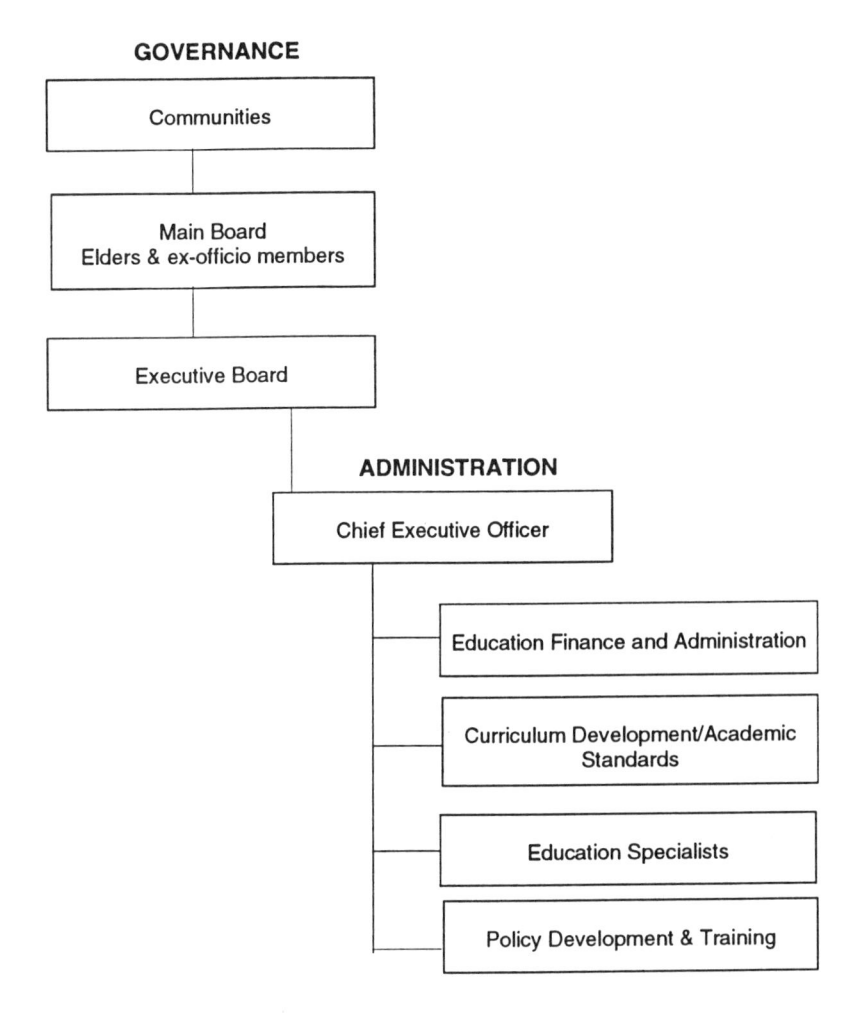

```
Chief Executive Officer
    |—— Education Finance and Administration
    |—— Curriculum Development/Academic Standards
    |—— Education Specialists
    |—— Policy Development & Training
```

Source: AFN 1995. Education Framework Agreement: Transition Team Report. Winnipeg: AFN.

Figure 8: Proposed New Education Structure for Manitoba

The developments taking place in the funding of First Nations education in Manitoba, Nova Scotia and in the other provinces represent a long and hard-fought battle for control of First Nations affairs, as well as the development of policy making. Downey (1988) describes policy as "an authoritative determination by a governing authority . . . and an authoritative allocation of resources" (p. 10). He further states that "policy-making is a purely political process . . . power and influence-based positions" (p. 18). It is noted that education funding for First Nations could either be policy instruments of domination and control or instruments of self-determination, not both. Perhaps another perspective can be examined. If one takes the incremental view of policy making, then financing First Nations education in Canada may be viewed as a long incremental struggle for a people to control their own lives; something that other Canadians have long had since 1867. After all, the principle of equality is a long-standing and very important part of the Canadian tradition. Yet this principle that embodies the concept of fairness and justice was denied the Aboriginal people. The symbiotic linkage of colonial politics and education in support of the prevailing ideologies, socio-economic and political order cannot be excused for the dysfunctional effects upon First Nations, as this legacy of control, exclusion and neglect remains with us today. Perhaps with the devolution movement taking place across Canada and changes in federal policies, First Nations will begin to acquire and control the financial resources that they need to bring their people into fully participating citizens in the Canadian mosaic.

References

Assembly of Manitoba Chiefs (1995). *Education framework agreement transition Team report.* Winnipeg, MB.

AMC Assembly of Manitoba Chiefs (1991). Indian education funding study: Final Report. Winnipeg, MB: AMC

Assembly of First Nations (1988). *Tradition and education: Towards a vision of our future.* Ottawa, ON: AFN.

Battiste, M and Barman, J. (Eds.) (1995). *First Nations education in Canada: The circle unfolds.* Vancouver, BC: UBC Press.

Binda K.P. (1997, June). "A comparative perspective on Maori education in New Zealand and Aboriginal education in Canada," Paper Presented at the Annual Meeting of the Comparative and International Education Society of Canada, St. John's Newfoundland.

Binda, K.P. (1996, January). "Equality through community control of Aboriginal eeducation in Canada," Paper Presented at the World Council for Curriculum and Instruction – 8th Triennal World Conference on Education, Amristar, India.

Binda, K.P. (1995). "Perceptions of local control in a First Nations tribal community," *McGill Journal of Education, 30* (2), 199-209.

Burns, G.E. (1996, June). "Native control of Native education in First Nations/provincial school boards tuition agreement negotiations and tuition agreement education," Paper Presented at the Annual Meeting of the Comparative and International Education Society of Canada, St. John's, Newfoundland.

Burns, G.E. (1996, November). Native control of Native education in provincial school boards/First Nations tuition agreement, negotiations and tuition agreement schooling. Paper Presented at the Assembly of First Nations National Conference on Education, Winnipeg, Manitoba.

Cassidy, M. (1992). *Overview of the First Round.* Ottawa, ON: Ontario: Royal Commission on Aboriginal Peoples.

Chretien, J. (1969). *Statement of the government of Canada on Indian policy.* Ottawa, ON: INAC

Chretien, J. (1972). "A venture in Indian education: Minister's address to the Council of Ministers of Education, Canada." Regina, Saskatchewan.

Common, R. and Frost, L., (1994). *Teaching wigwams: A modern vision of Native education.* Muncey, ON: Anishinable Kendaaswin Publishing.

Department of Indian Affairs and Northern Development (1982). Indian Education paper: Phase I. Ottawa, ON: DIAND.

Downy, L.W. (1988). *Policy analysis in education.* Calgary, AB: Detselig Enterprises.

Harris, M. (1975). *Culture, people, nature: An introduction to general anthropology.*

Hawthron, H.B. (Ed.) (1967). *A survey of the contemporary Indians of Canada.* Ottawa ON: INAC.

INAC/AMC (1994). *Framework agreement: Workplan, memorandum of understanding.* Winnipeg, MB: INAC-AMC.

INAC/AMC (1990). *Education framework agreement (EFA).* Winnipe, MB INAC-AMC.

INAC (1997a). *1997-1998 estimates: A report on plans and priorities.* Pilot document.

INAC (1997b). *Education management regime 1997/98.* Winnipeg, MB: INAC.

INAC (1997c). *Generic financial agreement* Ottawa: INAC.

INAC (1996a). *Performance paper improved reporting to parliament: Pilot document for the period ending March 31, 1996.* Ottawa, ON: INAC.

INAC (1996b). *Basic departmental data.* Ottawa, ON: INAC.

INAC (1995). *Year-end reporting handbook for DIAND funding agreements.* Ottawa, ON: INAC.

Irwin, R. (1997). "Speaking notes at the signing of an agreement with respect to Mi'Kmaq education in Nova Scotia." (http.//www.inac.gc.ca/) February, 14.

MacPherson, J.C. (1991). The MacPherson report on tradition and education: Towards a vision of our future. Ottawa, ON: DIAND.

Ministry of Colleges and Universities (1991). *Proposed Native education and training strategy.* Toronto, ON: Ministry of Education and Training, Province of Ontario.

Ministry of Education and Training (1994). *Aboriginal education and training strategy:* Annual Report for the Fiscal Year 1993-94 Toronto, ON: Author.

National Indian Brotherhood (AFN) (1972). *Indian control of Indian education.* Ottawa, ON: AFN.

Ontario Ministry of Education and Training (1993). *School boards/First Nations tuition agreements resource manual 1993/94* Toronto, ON: Author.

Royal Commission on Aboriginal Peoples (1996). *Report.* Ottaw, ON: RCAP.

Salasan Associates (1991). *Research report: Alternative funding arrangements.* Winnipeg, MB: Author.

Serson, S. (1996). Speaking notes for the Deputy Minister of INAC to the Public Accounts Committee, House of Commons, Ottawa. (http.//www/inac.gc.ca/) December, 10.

Schnitzer, M. (1990). *Information package for Indian communities contemplating local control of education.* Winnipeg, MB: INAC.

York, G. (1992). *The dispossessed: life and death in Native Canada.* Toronto, ON: Little Brown and Company.

Section Two

Possible Solutions and Prospects

6

Toward a Better Understanding of the Economic Contributions of the Public Schools

Y.L. Jack Lam

Introduction

To rectify the economic mismanagement of the last two decades, governments at both the federal and provincial levels are engaging in rigorous cost-cutting measures and downsizings. While reduction of national deficits that stands at about 573 billion now, seems a logical and a necessary step in putting the house in proper order, they have, unfortunately confused social investment from social cost. Public education from individual, organizational, social and national perspectives has always been viewed as an investment, an investment in human capital rather than public burden (Alexander, 1976; Shultz, 1961).

For elaboration, education on individual terms broadens the range of job opprotunities and offers some security against joblessness. One need only remember that in a period of slackening of business and industrial activities, it is the entrepreured educated individuals rather than large corporations that create jobs for themselves and others. Since 1988, there were 38 000 jobs lost in the public sector, 75 000 jobs lost in the manufacturing and construction areas and 1 195 000 jobs created in the retail, entertainment and financial services (Wells, 1996).

Statistics highlight another fact that the educational levels are highly related to income (Psacharopoulos, 1981; U.S. Department of Commerce, 1994). Even though there still is much gender inequity, the income increase is still highly related to the years of schooling one receives (see Figure 1). If one considers only the taxes paid by individuals who make more money, the benefit to the state is significant.

In the context of groups and community, education produces and extends benefit beyond the internal values obtained by its recipients. The quality of community life will be improved through appreciation of cultural activities, concerns for ecological balance and the reduction of crimes, poverty, dependency, and other social ills. Opponents to revenue increases for schools need to consider the high cost of supporting welfare recipients, many of whom are uneducated or under-educated to break into the job market. In the case of British Columbia, for instance, those who are unable to find jobs and continue to receive income assistance, an overwhelming proportion (i.e., over 60%) are those who have only high school education or less (Province of British Columbia, Ministry of Social Services, 1995). Ironically, the solution to this unemployable group to both the federal and provincial governments is re-education and retraining.

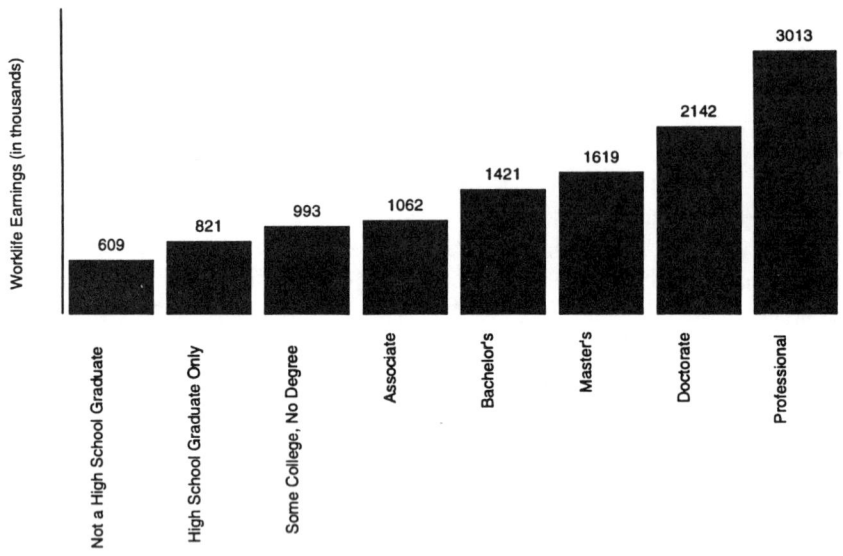

[Bar chart: Worklife Earnings (in thousands) by education level — Not a High School Graduate: 609; High School Graduate Only: 821; Some College, No Degree: 993; Associate: 1062; Bachelor's: 1421; Master's: 1619; Doctorate: 2142; Professional: 3013]

Source: Bureau of the Census Statistical Brief, August 1994, U.S. Department of Commerce, Economic and Statistics Administration, Bureau of the Census, p. iii.

Figure 1: Worklife Earnings in Thousands by Level of Education

In the context of social upward progress and advancement, education is undoubtedly a major propelling force. One way of measuring this aspect is the percentage of total human efforts that is being diverted to production of the material goods required for survival, such as food, clothing and shelter versus the efforts devoted to the producing nonmaterial goods that make life more comfortable (Burrup, Brimley & Garfield, 1996). Societies at the lower end of the social-progress continuum devote all or nearly all their efforts to producing essential material goods. As societies move up the scale of civilization, the percentage of human effort expended to produce services and goods not required for subsistence increases. In Canada, between 1981 and 1991, agriculture employed 4% of the work force while employment from other primary and manufacturing industries which declined substantially in the ten years makes up only 1% of the Canadian work force. Employment from the construction segment was 6% and manufacturing industries, whose work force has declined rapidly, constituted only 14% (Research sub-committee, 1995). On the other hand, all service industries combined had evolved to be the largest employers in all areas of Canada (Figure 2). They accounted between 70% to 73% of employment in the ten provinces. In the Northwest Territories and Yukon, the percentage was even higher (i.e., 81%).

Employment growth, 1981 to 1991, by industry (%)

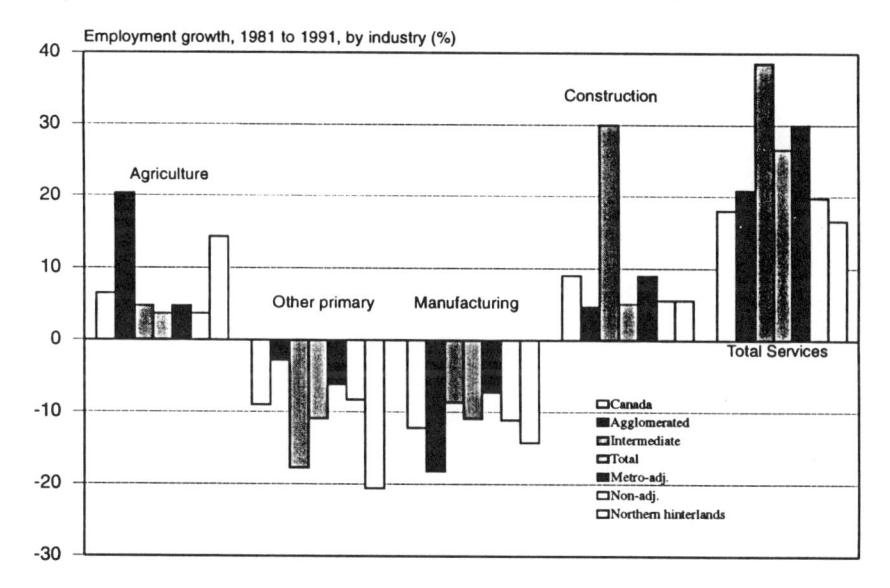

Source: Statistics Canada, Census of Population, 1991.

Figure 2: Employment Growth Rates Strongest in Service Industries

In a national context, education stimulates economic growth. Of the five factors that are responsible for the creation of national wealth – labor, capital, technology, resources and management – all are enhanced through education (Burrup, Brimley & Garfield, 1996). Educated workers are more skilled, take more pride in their work, are able to do a better job, faster and more creatively than less educated workers. Education equips workers with greater ability to produce and better opportunities to fulfil organizational and personal needs.

The shifting of World Bank positions from the financial investments in physical assets such as ports, roads, irrigation dames, factories and machines to loans for education demonstrate a recognition of education as a primary investment in human capitals which are critical for substaining agricultural, manufacturing and technological developments.

In 1992, a comprehensive report prepared by the Economic Council of Canada, entitled "A Lot To Learn" was released, stressing that

> To succeed in fiercely competitive global markets (Chapman & Walberg, 1992), Canadians will have to be innovative and flexible enough to exploit new technologies. This means that they must have good foundation skills and that they must continually extend and upgrade their range of specialized skills. In addition, however, it is clear that the new skill requirements placed a heavy premium on scientific and technological literacy.

It further recommends that more of the top Canadian graduates in science and mathematics must be attracted to the pursuit of advanced studies in order to be among the innovators and developers of the future, a point further stressed by the Committee on National Standards in Education (1994) when it focuses on the need to raise the performance of students for the benefit of the nation.

Conflicting Messages From the Governments

Yet, it seems highly incomprehensible that given the evidence that education provides some kind of safe net for employment, increase individual potential for earning capacity, and stimulate economic growth, the government chooses to ruthlessly trim the education budgets, causing possible deterioration of the quality of their education system and then, ironically, pour additional resources to repair the damages done by providing additional education and retraining for school dropouts who consititute the majority of the unemployed and welfare recipients.

Given the evidence that education generates social and community externalities – preserving social order and reduction of crime, most of the provincial governments between 1993-94 and 1994-5 reduce educational budgets by 2-3% while the federal government increases its spending on correctional services (including penitentiary and parole services from $934 000 000 to $975 000 000. This represents a 4% increase in operational expenditures and a 15% increase in capital expenditures (Public Accounts of Canada, 1993-94, 1994-95).

Some Probable Causes

Why is it that Governments at all levels are addressing the symptoms of the problems while at the same time dismembering the basic investment in education? Why are they willing to sacrifice long term benefits for short term gains?

The probable reasons are to be located in the political, economic and educational areas. From the political perspective, all governments are living on short mandates and require instant results to appease their constituencies without worrying about the long term effects. With public education cost continuing to rise, and with the apparent tolerance of the taxpayers for another round of tax hikes seemingly reaching a limit, it would seem that the logical step is to cut back on all expenditures including funding of the school systems. This seems to the author to be an authentic consideration.

From the economic perspective, aside from the urgent need to address national debt, two principles seem to provide some frame of reference in explaining government actions. The first is the marginal dollar principle which examines whether additional resources to be chanelled into education would increase the productivity of the school system or whether the resources should be used for other services or goods. The second economic principle is the point of diminishing returns, i.e., a point beyond which additional expenditures will yield very little or no additional educational returns (Burrup, Brimley, & Garfield, 1996). Unlike areas such as agriculture and medicine, greatly increased expenditures for education have not, cannot, and will not produce such large or fantastic increases or improvements in its products. Nonetheless, there is no government documents, to the best knowledge of the author, that exist which outline these economic analyses as the deciding factors in their continued cutback on funding for public education.

From the educational perspective, various reform movements both in Canada and in United States aim at higher productivity from the instructional staff, lower administration costs, better utilization of building and resources and other cost-saving remedies (Hanushek, 1989; Monk, 1990; Pipho, 1993). However, the cost-quality relationship in education is hard to be established in view of the lack of consensus in terms of the educational outcomes, the lack of common criteria, and the difficulty of ascertaining efficiency, which tends to destroy public confidence in social and governmental institutions.

Associated with the non-tangible educational processes and outcomes are the limitations and lack of success in educational research in this domain. While some of the research seem to recognize that there is a positive relationship between cost and quality in education and various foundation programs that provincial governments use in allocating resources implicitly acknowledge quality of education is associated with regional willingness to spend, there is no common agreement in the research findings to unequivably verify this postulation.

New Empirical Evidence Supporting Education as Investment

In response to general confusion on the part of the governments treating education as expenditure than investment, to the misconceived notion of the public that education is an eating machine, a devourer of tax revenues, constantly consuming public monies giving little or nothing in return (Bedenbaugh, 1985), and to the limited success that education research has in identifying concrete and tangible impacts that the funding of the public school has, the writer of this chapter undertakes a study assessing the economic and social impacts that the public education has upon rural communities in Manitoba. In some way, this study brings to the skeptic public a step closer to a better understanding of the of the tangible economic and social roles education plays, that has hitherto been illusive to them.

Over the past three decades, there has been a severe and steady rural depopulation among the Prairie Provinces. By examining the census taken between 1960-90, about 124 rural communities in Saskatchewan, 118 in Alberta and 84 in Manitoba have disappeared or cease to exist as functional communities. To many, this does not signify the decline of agriculture as a primary industry in the Prairie Provinces. Indeed agriculture remains vibrant in these regions despite fluctuation in crop prices in the world (Figure 3). Rather, it is the slow but steady deterioration of the infrastructure of rural communities brought about by short-sighted need to economize, forcing the disappearance of rail, post, and recently regional medical centres that precipitates out-migration from the rural communities.

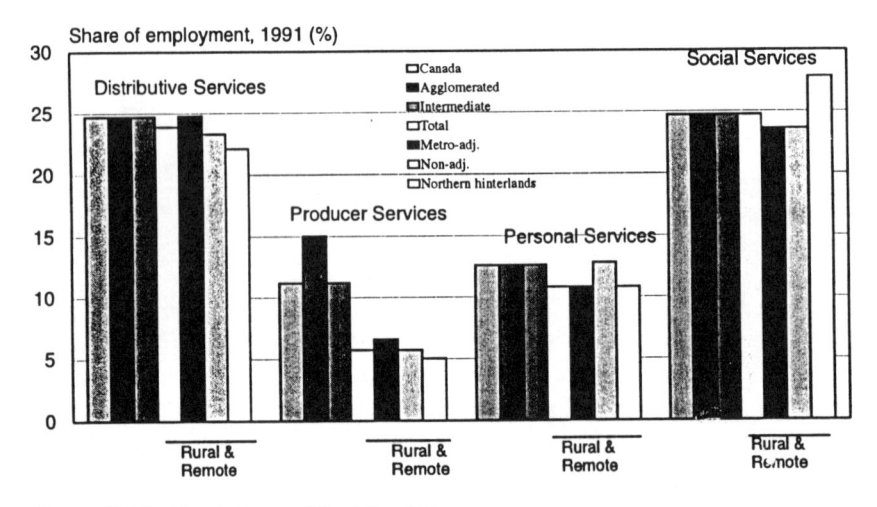

Share of employment, 1991 (%)

Legend: □Canada, ■Agglomerated, ■Intermediate, □Total, ■Metro-adj., □Non-adj., □Northern hinterlands

Categories: Distributive Services, Producer Services, Personal Services, Social Services (each shown for Rural & Remote)

Source: Statistics Canada, Census of Population, 1991

Figure 3: Rural Share of Employment in Services, Low Only in Producer Services

Rural depopulation, to some, may just signify the inevitable change of time. To many, however, it does represent a loss of an important part of Canadian culture and heritage, a radical uprooting of a traditional lifestyle, a growing disparity in regional development, and to the present Manitoba Government, an erosion of its power base as most of the members of legislative assembly come from rural constituencies.

Sensing the gravity of the situation, both the federal government and the Government of Manitoba attempt to revitalize rural economoy in a number of programs:

The Federal Government initiates Western Economic Diversification Program in order to discourage over-dependence on a single economy which will be highly vulnerable to the world market prices. I had the opportunity to assess the effectiveness of this program. Of the 38 Manitoba rural communities contacted, I had to conclude the program is of limited utility. Slightly over half viewed this program as "not useful." The major problems expressed were that the program is "poorly organized"; it is geared to larger centres" and "not in touch with reality."

The Manitoba Government initiates Rural Grow Bonds. The purpose of this program is to provide investment funds for rural economic undertaking. An overwhelming 66% of the surveyed communities rated this program as "not useful" again. The major complaints from the community leaders were that the program was highly restrictive in nature with a set of criteria "narrowly defined." They further commented that the officials running the program were highly bureaucratic. When the rural enterprises supported by the bonds fail, as in the recent case in Portage la Prairie, the public investment is lost (Lam & Haque, 1994).

The second initiative by the Manitoba government was the decentralization of government structure so that more employees will be relocated and reassigned to rural community. Such an effort, from the viewpoints of the community leaders are at best partially successful. There was too much pressure from the Public Service Employee Union to make this campaign promise truly beneficial. The disappointment experienced by some community was compounded by the closure of some government agencies, i.e., regional water resource departments and employment services centres.

The third initiative by the Manitoba government, REDI (The Rural Economic Development Initiative), is to

> utilize the fund generated completely from the video lottery terminals in rural Manitoba to support business development, strengthen rural infrastructure, promote conservation, environmental industries, tourism development, commercial and water and gas projects and export service activities. In addition, this program provides business loan guarantees, conducts business seminars, and mentorship for high school students. As in the case of all the previous government initiative, it was received by the surveyed communities in a lukewarm manner. (Lam & Haque, 1994)

In 1993, The Manitoba Government through the Rural Development Institute of Brandon University instructed that a project to investigate the economic opportunities for immigrants in rural Manitoba be undertaken, and the writer was asked to be the chief investigator of the project. The explicit intention of this project was to access the infrastructure of the rural communities, and to detect how receptive rural communities were with respect to different types of new immigrants. The implicit intention was to see if Manitoba could attract more immigrant investors to revitalize rural communities. Currently the inflow of investment from immigrants into Canada is about two billion dollars per year. Most of the investors' money has gone to B.C. and Ontario. Manitoba is anxious to increase its portion from the current $145 million.

Results of the survey and interviews with mayors and chairs of the chambers of commerce of the 64 communities (Lam & Haque, 1994) indicated they were ready and willing to accept immigrants, particularly investor immigrants. However, the infrastructure of these communities are in varying stages of capabilities in attracting this class of immigrants. Given that some communities are quite far from markets, some have inadequacy of power sources, some have no pool of technical manpower, some do not have raw materials, and all suffer from geographical isolation and severity of winter climate, it is highly unlikely that large corporations will establish their operations in most of the rural communities. If so, the continued search for capital infusion either from immigrant investors or from the established businesses is chasing a pie in the sky.

Ironically, to the oversight or total unawareness of the Manitoba Government, through its support for rural school divisions, amounting to no less than $300 million a year (Manitoba Education and Training, School Finance Branch, 1991-92; Lam, 1996), it has already created a mega-project which plays a major role in stablizing rural economy. What is lacking at the present moment is the collection and analysis of empirical data that will provide concrete and precise information in guiding the reconceptualization of the public school as a vehicle in promoting regional economic well-being.

In contrast to the earlier argument that education has beneficial effects on individuals, communities and the nation as a whole, which to the public is "intangible" in their short-term perspective, Lam's study of the impact of the public school on rural communities (1996) yields concrete and tangible evidence that as a public institution, the school plays a key role both in the economic and social well-beings of the rural communities.

In brief, the four rural school divisions encompassing eight rural communities constituted the sample of the study. The choice of the rural communities was guided by the assumption that the effects of the public schools would be most lucidly manifested when there was only one or two schools in the communities. Thus the chosen rural communities were all small, with the population not more than 1 000 people.

In terms of budget, these four rural school divisions receive about 65-70% of $41 000 000 from the provincial government every year to support their operation and this should be viewed as typical of all other rural school divisions. Of the 80% of the school division budget that were primarily personnel salaries, it was found that some 50% of the educational fundings was retained in the rural communities either as the school staff's support for local business or as personal savings in the local banks or credit unions. About 30% of the personnel income spent in the neighboring communities and only a small fraction, i.e., 10%, of the income was spent in urban centres. The noted spending patterns account a great deal for the continued existence and the stability of many local business and service industries in rural communities (Figure 4).

Two interesting points must be underscored in analyzing the spending patterns of the school staff. First, unless the needed commodities are unavailable from the local shops, the school staff seldom spent their money in urban centres. While this might reflect, to some extent, the geographical isolation of rural communities, making long shopping trips undesirable, the spending patterns often register a deliberate political choice of supporting local business even though the commodities could be higher price-wise than urban centres and the selection is limited. Interviews with the school personnel and local business managers confirmed such a choice rests on the acute awareness of the importance of mutual support for survival.

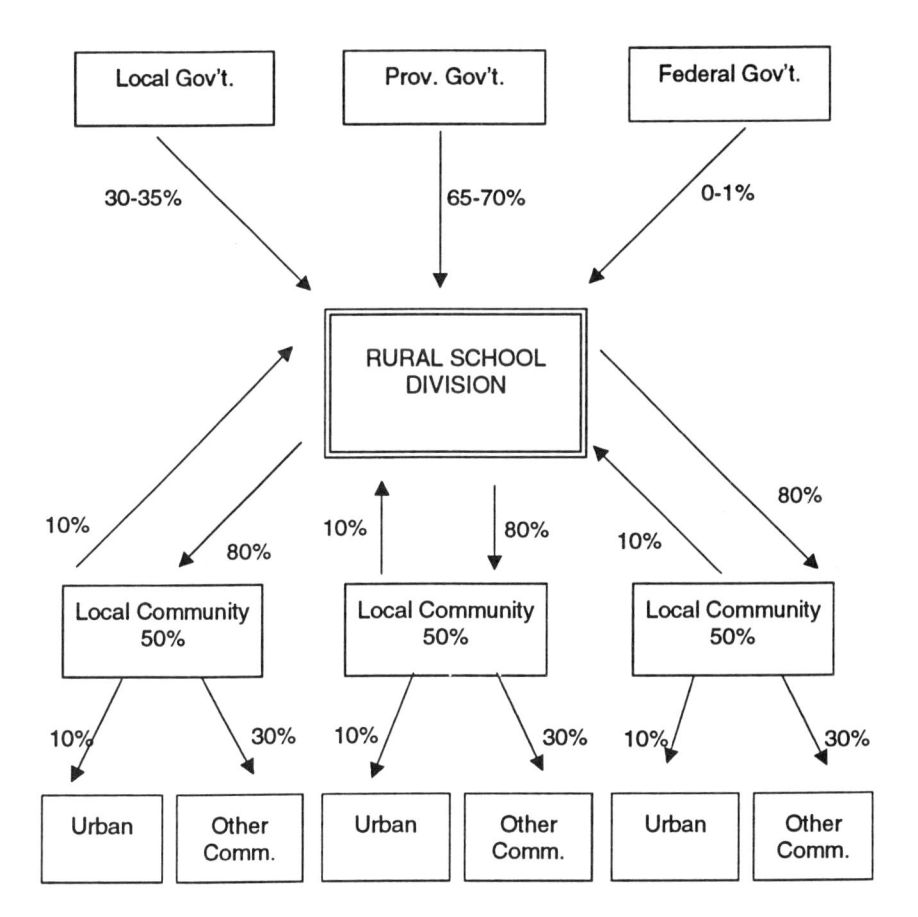

```
                    Local Gov't.         Prov. Gov't.          Federal Gov't.

                       30-35%              65-70%                 0-1%

                              RURAL SCHOOL
                                DIVISION

                                                                    80%
         10%              10%        80%           10%
                 80%
      Local Community      Local Community        Local Community
           50%                  50%                    50%

      10%       30%       10%       30%         10%       30%
    Urban     Other     Urban     Other       Urban     Other
              Comm.               Comm.                 Comm.
```

Figure 4: Typical Cash Flow in Four Rural School Divisions

Second, that 30% of the staff's salaries are spent on other rural centres (usually, larger communities where the school division offices are most likely located), suggests a close linkage between individual rural communities and their rural centres. Lam's study (1996) analogises such close connections as spokes radiating from the centre of the wheel (i.e. the rural centre with which individual communities develop close economic connections). Should the isolated rural communities die, the spokes of the wheel rot and the whole region will slowly but steadily sink into a state of economical depression.

Aside from the direct economic contribution that the public school makes to the rural communities, Lam's study also revealed the social impact that the public school has on the surveyed communities. When parents, who constitute 32-36% of the total population of the surveyed communities were approached to respond to the extent they utilized the school buildings for various social functions, they indicated that the premises were only moderately used for those purposes. However, when they were asked to rate the importance of the school to them and to their communities, almost all respondents rated the school as "important" to "very important." When they were further approached to respond to question of how the presence of the school affect their decision to stay or move away from the communities, a very significant proportion indicated that their mobility would be largely dependent on the presence or disappearence of the school.

Again, one can identify two important aspects from the feedback of parents. One, parents' strong alliance with the public school in rural area have given rise to so many political battles with their school boards which have the inclination to take a direct, expedient, but ill-conceived approach of closing schools (Lam, 1982) when they experience enrolment decline, a phenomenon not uncommon in rural regions. In most situations, the concerned school boards will deem these schools as economically "unviable." What the board members do not realize is that when they close rural schools, they have jeopardized the existence of the community affected (Fedo, 1972; Holland, Baritelle & White, 1976).

Second, given that the majority of the parents in the rural communities hinge their final decision to stay on or move away from the communities, school closure will accerlerate the depopulation process that is taking place in the Prairie Provinces. On the other hand, the presence of the school in rural communities tend to stabilize the demographic shift and curtail the inequity in regional development.

In this context, one can sense that even with the special levy imposed on local properties, to generate 30-35% of the total education expenditure for the four school divisions, which is not a light taxation in view of the present-day financial plight of the rural communities, most of the community members were willing to endure this burden without too much protest,

Conclusion

Amidst the general rush to bring about balanced budget and reduction of national and provincial debts, there is a tendency for both the federal and provincial governments to forget or overlook the fact that public education is NOT primarily a service to be treated in the same context as medical care or other social services. To do so is to ignore all the past research examining the impact of education on individual lifetime earning capacity, on community lifestyle improvement, on social welfare reduction and crime prevention and on national productivity and its international competitiveness.

A more appropriate vision is to perceive education as a sensible form of human investment that should reap individual and collective benefits both from the short and long term perspectives. Lacking such a vision, as in the case of all the governments at the present time, lead to conflicting and discordent public policies that tend to confuse or antagonize their constituencies. While this might not be a political suicide for parties in power, it has certainly shaken our trust in our political structure in general and the politicians in particular.

Furthermore, inconsistency in public policies raises many fundamental questions about the logic of the governments' actions. Does it make good sense cutting back on public education funding, crippling the school's ability to educate properly all streams of students while increasing spending on the retraining of school dropouts and welfare recipients so as to ensure that these people, have a better chance to rejoin the labor market? Does it make good sense cutting back on public education that prepares individuals to live a decent life while adding substantial expenditure on penitentiaries to house the socially misfits? In the domain of rejuvenating rural regional development, does it make good sense for the government to dismantle in stages a well-established mega-project, namely, public education system, while pouring money to create incentive grants to attract wishful projects to stabilize rural economy or hoping against hope for some immigrant investors to initiate job-creation enterprises?

While the lack of proper vision about public education as a human investment might be attributed in the past to the absence of immediate and tangible effects of education, beyond what the politicians' term of office can visualize, emerging data of the economic and social impacts of the public school on rural communities, albeit a small sample that requires further amplification and investigation to generalize, provide urgency for the governments to re-examine the public education in a more proper perspective. Indeed, it is through the embracing of this proper vision that a more coherent set of public policies and actions would be put in place and further squandering of public funds on symptoms rather than the roots of the social problems can be avoided.

References

Alexander, K. (1976). "The value of an education," *Journal Of Education Finance, 1,* 429-467.

Bedenbaugh, E.H. (1985). "Education is still a good investment," *The Clearing House, 59,* 134-136.

British Columbia, Ministry of Social Services (1995). *A profile of income assistant clients who return to the caseload.* Victoria, BC: Government of British Columbia.

Bururp, P.E., Brimley, V. Jr. & Garfield, R.R. (1996). *Financing education in a climate of change.* 6th Edition. Boston, MA: Allyn & Bacon.

Chapman D.W. & Walberg. J. (eds.) (1992). *Advances in educational productivity: international perspective on educational productivity vol. 2.*

Committee on National Standards in Education (1994). *National standards in education: A question of excellence.* Report of the National Advisory Board on Science and Technology. Ottawa, ON: Government of Canada.

Economic Council of Canada (1992). *A lot to learn: Education and training in Canada.* Ottawa, ON: Economic Council of Canada.

Fedo, M.W. (1972). "The school that saved a town," *American Education, 8,* 6-9.

Hanushek, E.A. (1989). "The impact of differential expenditures on school performance," *Educational Researcher, 5,* 45-51.

Holland, D., Baritelle, J., & White, G. (1976). "School consolidation in sparsely populated rural areas: A case study," *Educational Administrative Quarterly, 12,* 67-79.

Lam, Y.L.J. (1982). "School closure: An answer to declining enrolment?" *Educational Horizons, 60,* 111-114.

Lam Y.L.J., & Haque, C.E. (1994). *Economic development and immigrant employment opportunities in rural Manitoba.* RDI report series no. 8. Brandon, MB: Rural Development Institute, Brandon University.

Lam, Y.L.J. (1996). The economic and social impacts of public schools on rural communities. RDI report series No. 8. Brandon, MB: Rural Development Institute, Brandon University.

Monk, D. (1990). Educational finance: An economic approach. New York, NY: McGraw Hill.

Pipho, C. (1993). "School finance: moving from quity to productivity," *Phi Delta Kappan, 4,* 590-91.

Public Accounts of Canada (1993-4). Summary report and financial statements. Ottawa, ON: Government of Canada.

Public Accounts of Canada (1994-5). Summary report and financial statements. Ottawa, ON: Government of Canada.

Psacharopoulos, G., (1981). "Return to education: An updated international comparison," *Comparative Education, 17,* 321-341.

Research Subcommittee of the Interdepartmental Committee on Rural and Remote Canada (1995). Rural Canada: A profile. Ottawa, ON: Government of Canada.

Sher, U.P., & Tompkins, R.B., (1977). "Economy, efficiency and equality: The myth of rural school district consolidation," *Council Of Educational Facility Planners Journal, 4,* 14.

Shultz, T.W. (1961). "Investment in human capital," *American Economic Review, 51,* 1-17.

Swanson, A.D. & King, R.A. (1991). *School finance: Its economics and Pplitics.* New York, NY: Longman.

U.S. Department of Agriculture (1990-91). *Rural conditions and trends,* Washington, DC: U.S. Dept. of Agriculture.

U.S. Department of Commerce (1994). Bureau of the Census Statistical Brief. Washington, DC, U.S. Dept. of Commerce.

Wells, J. (1996, March). "Jobs" *Maclean's,* 12-16.

7

Promoting Equity, Adaptability and Efficiency in Public School Systems through Alternative Resource Allocation

Stephen B. Lawton

Educators across Canada feel like they have been hit by a freight train. After travelling the same path for five decades, building one of the world's most extensive educational systems, they now see significant portions of their handiwork under attack or lying in ruins.

At Dalhousie, it was a bulldozer, not a freight train, that demolished the building of the former of faculty of education, once home to The Atlantic Institute of Education which had been founded by Dr. Robert Jackson, first director The Ontario Institute for Studies in Education, after his retirement. The Atlantic Institute, closed a decade ago not long after Dr. Jackson's tragic death, and the Dalhousie faculty of education had offered the only doctoral programs in education in the Atlantic provinces. Their demise is symbolic of the changes now transforming education in Canada. Both confidence in the visions of post-war educationists and the resources to support them have declined. In the desperate fight for survival, the question of how education is funded has become paramount.

Funding education has at least three critical components: revenue, which concerns where money comes from; expenditure, how much is spent; and allocation, or how the money is spent. In the current climate of restraint, three criteria are appropriate in judging the success of a funding system: equity, which concerns the fairness of the system to students; adaptability, the extent to which the educational system accommodates changing conditions; and efficiency, gaining the most value for the funds used. These components and criteria are linked to the vision of education that is being delivered through a process for translating public policy into public service.

The vision held of education is critical since different visions imply different types, amounts, and allocations of resources. The transformation in public education in the post-war period reflected the transition from the "little red school house" to the large, complex public school board with its many large schools, specialized professionals, and divisions devoted to a wide range of more effective teaching, and greater opportunities for its children. With the introduction of new educational philosophies and practices, children were to experience not only better lives in material terms, but better lives in terms of their individual fulfilment. The current commitment of citizens to this vision of education is critical to the question of funding: when people believe in a vision, they will sacrifice for it; when they begin to doubt, they will question these sacrifices; when they lose faith they will turn elsewhere. I believe that, today, many people, particularly parents, are beginning to doubt the post-war vision of education. Other visions may promise more; other visions may cost less.

Revenue – "During a drought, animals at the water hole look at one another differently."

In the competition for funds at the public trough, public education maintains a strong position. Surveys indicate that more spending on public education is preferred by a majority of Canadians; education stands second only to health care in this regard. But even a strong position cannot compensate for the decline in the level of resources available for all public programs. Even though Canada – the federal government, provinces, and territories – have total revenues today that are the greatest in its history, a smaller proportion of those funds are available for publicly financed goods and services.

Figure 1 portrays the growth in public expenditures between 1984 and 1994 combining all levels of public expenditures; Figure 2 depicts the growth in public debt between 1977 and 1995. Figure 1 displays federal expenditures on both programs and on servicing the federal debt between 1966 and 1995. It is evident that expenditures on debt have been increasing more rapidly than program expenditures. The continuation of deficit financing – spending more in a year than a government collects – at a federal level and in the two largest provinces (which account for almost 60% of Canada's population) means that expenditures to pay for interest on our collective debt continue to grow. Today, that debt amounts to approximately $100 000 for a family of four, an amount larger than the average home mortgage. Per capita interest on this public debt is almost $2 500 per year.

Increasingly, our governments have had to turn to others to raise funds needed to fund public services and pay interest on debt. Now, approximately 40% of the debt is owed to other nations, often in foreign currencies – yen, deutsche marks, Swiss francs, and U.S. dollars. The debt and the composition of our lenders have two pernicious effects. Government deficits and refinancing create a demand for money that increases interest rates, which is the "price" of money; as always, when the demand for something increases, its price increases. High interest rates mean reduced investments, lower sales of houses and automobiles and, thus, higher unemployment. Also, the external nature of the debt means that uneasy investors may, at any time, withdraw their money from Canada. When a currency is "dumped" on the international currency markets, its value is forced down. To resist this trend, the central bank may raise interest rates in order to make the currency more attractive to investors. Again, the effects of the high interest rates ripple out to weaken the economy.

	1984			1994[a]		
	Federal	Consolidated prov.-local	Consolidated all gov't.	Federal	Consolidated prov.-local	Consolidated all gov't.
	millions of dollars					
General services	4,487	7,235	11,714	7,562	12,041	19,603
Protection of persons and property	9,866	5,743	15,232	15,822	11,106	26,248
Transportation and communications	3,190	8,381	11,383	3,789	12,703	16,317
Health	6,197	23,478	24,096	8,331	48,846	47,820
Social services	31,778	14,003	42,186	59,458	33,587	85,616
Education	3,565	24,321	24,869	4,914	42,685	44,420
Resource conservation and industrial development	8,751	6,171	14,194	6,683	8,986	14,573
Environment	486	3,169	3,633	751	7,315	8,049
Recreation and culture	805	3,330	4,134	1,347	6,000	7,328
Labour, employment and immigration	1,204	299	1,483	2,689	851	3,487
Housing	1,654	666	2,303	2,135	1,776	3,910
Foreign affairs and international assistance	1,743	---	1,743	3,924	---	3,924
Regional planning and development	224	788	1,010	485	1,233	1,706
Research establishments	1,188	173	1,361	1,584	350	1,934
Debt charges	18,054	10,864	28,839	37,982	26,820	64,739
General purpose transfers to other governments	6,560	---	---	11,460	---	---
Other	3,209	2,177	5,386	2,123	2,956	5,086
Total expenditure	102,961	110,798	193,566	171,039	215,254	354,761

[a] Estimate.
Sources: Trett & Cook, 1995

Figure 1: Government Expenditures, All Levels, Fiscal Years Ending Nearest to March 31, 1984 and March 31, 1994

Like any debtor wishing to reestablish good credit, there is only one solution to this problem: spend less on goods and services, and more on debt repayment. Collectively, this means spending less on public services, including education.

There are, of course, some who argue a different position, holding that the Bank of Canada could lower interest rates to stimulate our economy, while imposing exchange controls on money, and wage and price controls on the workers and businesses, in order to prevent inflation. This is a policy option (Canadian Centre for Policy Alternatives, 1995). We experienced wage and price controls in the 1970s and early 1980s; and the U.S.S.R. existed for the better part of this century with a state-run economy. Forbidding the open exchange of the Canadian dollar, however, would drive away foreign investors

Year	Federal	Provincial and territorial	Local	Consolidated net debt	Net debt as a % of GDP[a]	Net debt per capita[b]
	millions of dollars				%	$
1977	35,295	8,701	12,973	56,969	28.78	2,402
1978	45,615	10,059	14,117	69,791	32.04	2,912
1979	58,801	10,051	15,937	84,789	35.10	3,502
1980	72,331	10,641	16,058	99,030	35.87	4,043
1981	84,672	12,833	16,576	114,081	36.81	4,598
1982	97,711	11,176	16,969	125,856	35.36	5,009
1983	125,625	20,599	18,139	164,363	43.89	6,473
1984	162,250	28,404	18,526	209,180	51.56	8,161
1985	204,108	35,410	18,535	258,053	58.02	9,974
1986	239,888	48,935	19,020	307,843	64.41	11,784
1987	270,873	61,864	19,286	352,023	69.61	13,309
1988	298,103	70,007	20,221	388,331	70.40	14,499
1989	326,484	72,811	20,407	419,702	70.40	15,402
1990	354,848	75,850	19,575	450,273	69.27	16,273
1991	386,785	83,501	20,909	491,195	69.20	17,527
1992	421,316	108,669	22,050	552,035	81.81	19,475
1993	461,685	138,866	23,121[c]	623,672[c]	90.60[c]	21,757[c]
1994	503,766	161,717[d]	25,333[c]	690,816[c]	97.07[c]	23,768[c]
1995	543,063[c]	181,695[c]	[e]	[e]	[e]	[e]

[a] GDP for the calendar year ending in the fiscal year. [b] Population on April 1. [c] Estimate. [d] Revised estimate. [e] Not available.
Source: Statistics Canada, *Public Sector Finance*, 1994-1995, catalogue no. 68-212.

Figure 2: Federal, Provincial, and Local Goverrnment Net Debt on an FMS Basis on March 31, 1977 to 1995

and limit travel and investment options for Canadians. In short, there are "solutions" that are worse than the problem. Unfortunately, the gullible believe these "solutions" are viable options; they are misled to believe that there is an easy way out. It is this type of thinking – the notion that running annual federal deficits of $35 billion really doesn't matter – that got us into this predicament in the first place. Even Tommy Douglas, founder of the Canadian Commonwealth Federation, precursor to the New Democratic Party, warned that if government borrowed too much from banks, the banks would run the government.

The problems our governments face with debts and deficits are driving the fiscal agendas of the federal government and most provinces. Figure 2 displays the annual per capita deficits for each of the provinces for the 1990s. It is encouraging that over half the provinces have, at least from 1995-1996, balanced their budgets. Unfortunately, more restraint is in store.

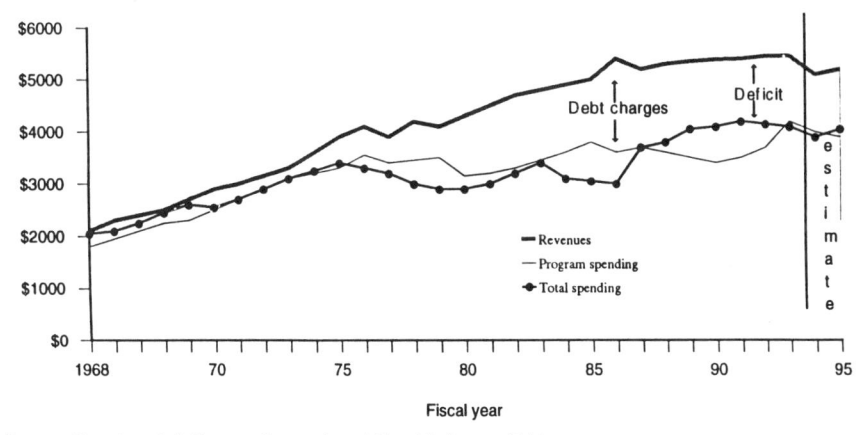

[Figure: line chart showing Revenues, Program spending, and Total spending from 1968 to 1995, with $ values from $0 to $6000. Arrows indicate "Debt charges" and "Deficit". Right side labeled "estimate".]

Source: Department of Finance, Economic and Fiscal Reference Tables

Figure 3: What Revenue Shortage? Real Federal Spending and Revenues, per Capita ($ = 1993)

What many do not realize is that federal and provincial deficits are balanced by transfer payments to provinces, municipalities and school boards, and people. Grants are transferred down the chain, and deficits are transferred up the chain. While a school board may claim that it has a "balanced budget," it should realized that part of the funds transferred to it by its province are borrowed. In Ontario, an average of 40% of school funds are paid by the province; in others, such as New Brunswick and Newfoundland, it is 100%. When a province gives a school board a grant, the school board "gives" the province a "debt"; if the province does not have sufficient revenue from provincial taxes and federal transfer payments to cover this "debt," it must borrow funds.

The impact of deficit reduction is clear; to spend less, the federal and provincial governments give less. Ultimately, the jurisdiction, institution, or individual that is "lowest on the food chain" suffers the consequences – and starts looking at others differently. With the federal government set to reduce its transfer payments by $2.6 billion from $29.7 billion to $26.9 billion in the 1996-97 fiscal year, provinces, school boards, universities, hospitals, and others must make decisions as to how they will cope with the impact these cuts (Government of Canada, 1995). Many have already prepared various scenarios, but until provinces announce their budgets for their next fiscal year, these institutions cannot act with certainty. Already, many of them have frozen hiring, announced lay-offs, ceased renewing contracts for services, and cancelled projects. Ontario's school boards, whose fiscal year began January 1, 1996, have taken anticipatory steps but will be well into their fiscal year before they can set final budgets and make firm decisions as to staffing.

The impact of federal cutbacks, which will continue with a further reduction of $1.8 billion for 1997-98, will differ in each province. Most federal transfer payments to provinces are contained in three programs, the general purpose equalization payments which are made to ensure that all provinces can afford a basic level of public services, the Established Programs Financing, which includes payments and tax points to pay for health care and postsecondary education, and the Canada Assistance Plan, to provide for welfare. The general purpose equalization payments have the effect of transferring revenue from the provinces with above average revenue-raising capacity (as measured by an index with over 20 possible revenue sources) to those with below average revenue capacity; that is, they transfer funds from British Columbia, Alberta, and Ontario to the seven other provinces. The latter two programs are to be combined into a Canada Social Transfer (CST) that "will free the provinces to pursue innovation by eliminating the restrictive cost-sharing feature of the Canada Assistance Plan" (p. 13). In the case of the Atlantic provinces, about 40% of the provincial revenue comes from these three federal transfer programs; in the case of Ontario, it is about 15%. Yet the dollar figures are largest in the larger provinces. Transfer payments to the Atlantic provinces total almost $5 billion, while those to Ontario and Quebec are about $7.5 billion each (Perry, 1995).

Restraints on provincial expenditures have caused elementary and secondary expenditures to level off since the early 1990s. In several provinces (Newfoundland, British Columbia, and Alberta, for example) governments have enacted legislation making the provincial government the sole source of school board revenue, a step earlier taken in both Prince Edward Island and New Brunswick. While Newfoundland abolished property and poll taxes for education, the others made their property tax into a provincial tax, albeit one collected locally in most cases. In other provinces, the portion of revenue for education from provincial sources has declined; dependence on the property tax has increased.

In Alberta, the province made widespread reductions across all sectors; elementary and secondary education made out relatively well, in fact, although the reductions amounted to 12.7% of the previous level of provincial funding. Provincial aid constituted about 50% of educational expenditures (before assumption of the property tax as provincial revenue), so the actual percent reduction was about 6.4%. Given that there was a 5% roll-back in wages accepted in the broader public sector in the province – which effects about 70% of the budget – the net reduction across school boards was effectively just 2.9%. This figure is arrived at as follows: 6.4% - (5% x .70) = 6.4% - 3.5% = 2.9%. The impact in some systems, especially the public board in Calgary, was much greater since the province also introduced a new funding system that equalized grants across the province; some boards lost up to 9%, while others gained up to 14%. This reallocation of revenue had as much impact on operations as did the overall level of reductions.

Expenditures – Where Does All the Money Go?

Listening to spokespersons for school boards, teachers' federations, school trustees and administrators, one might think that there has been a long downward spire in expenditures over the past two decades. In fact, nothing could be further from the truth. Overall, expenditures for public education steadily increased until the early 1990s, when provincial government first acted to get their financial houses in order. In an important paper, François Gendron (1994) gives a clear accounting of Canada's increasing investment in elementary and secondary education over two decades.

First, Gendron notes that in 1991, Canada spent 5% of its Gross Domestic Product (GDP) on education, tying with Sweden for first place among the developed nations represented in the Organization of Economic Cooperation and Development (OECD); the average figure was 3.9%. In 1991, Canadian expenditures on elementary and secondary education were $33.6 billion. Had it been spending at the OECD average level, its expenditures would have been $7.4 billion – or 22% – less. In fact, had Canada still been spending the same amount of money (after adjusting for inflation) that it had in 1971, it would have been spending $7.4 billion less! Where did this new money go?

According to Gendron, most of the funds went to maintain or increase staffing levels even while school enrolments were declining: "As these two trends moved in opposite directions, the student/educator ratio gradually decreased, from a high of 21 in 1971 to 15 by 1991 (p. 16)." This represents a 29% reduction in the number of students per educator. He notes that, "Contractual job security clauses and a school enrolment often distributed over large geographic areas prevent school administrators and government from quickly adjusting the size of the teaching forces to the number of students. Furthermore, new educational programs were added to school curricula, including the early 1970s launch of the federal government Official Languages in Education program, French immersion classes and second language education programs were created in all provinces, causing increased demand for new teachers. Special education programs and mainstreaming were also introduced. . . . (p.17). Also, although salaries for teachers at a given level increased only slightly faster than inflation (7.9% vs 7.5%), "many educators moved to higher salary categories, thereby increasing the overall average salary . . . from $10 029 in 1971 to $55 979 in 1991 . . . a 9% average annual increase (p. 14)."

Allocation – Who gets What and the Notion of "Relative Deprivation"

During the 1970s and 1980s, increases in education expenditures reflected governments' recognition of the need or desires of many different groups, as alluded to by Gendron. Many of these demands for recognition were based on claims for equity or social justice. Elementary teachers sought to "close the gap" between per student expenditures for elementary and secondary students; Roman Catholic school boards in provinces with separate school systems sought parity with their public counterparts; French-language communities demanded programs equal to those provide English-language students.

In many cases the objective situation at the classroom level did not exhibit striking disparities nor was there evidence that observed differences in achievement would respond to infusions of money. The problem was that someone else, who was perceived as being no better nor more deserving, was getting more. Samuel Stouffer, the American sociologist, coined a term for this sort of behavior: relative deprivation. While in reality little or no difference exists, a grievance grows so that the perception of even minor differences are accentuated in the mind. Similar problems are common in organizations where merit pay is given; the allocation of a hundred dollars per year more to one person than another sets off a feud that destroys morale and creates harm out of all proportion to the amount at issue. Jealously is a powerful emotion.

Equity is admittedly, an important value that coincides with our notions of fairness and justice. In large organizations, be the school boards or ministries of education, a key value is that equal treatment procedurally, one should not favour one individual or group over another. All should be equal before the law. But the claims of the 1970s and 1980s went well beyond even equal treatment, arguing that some groups have needs that demand entitlements greater than those due the average person. "Special students," either with greater learning needs or with unusual gifts, required tailored programs. Remote schools and school boards had needs that transcended the needs of the "average" school and school board. These types of claims received generous acknowledgement from governments at all levels. A recent study of expenditures in New York state revealed similar trends there; while overall expenditures increased 46% in real terms between 1980 and 1992, those for the average pupil actually declined. Full-time equivalent staff for special education increased 75%, while FTE for nonspecial education – facetiously termed the "severely normal" – declined by 2% (Lankford & Wycoff, 1995).

The claims for equitable treatment are particularly pernicious in the case of school board funding since the "ability" to pay traditionally is measured by a single value: the equalized assessed value (EAV) per student. Equalized assessment is the value of property in a jurisdiction adjusted for differing assessment practices to provide an estimate of its current market value. Divided by the number of pupils, this provides an index of a school board's "wealth." Figure 3 demonstrates the distribution of equalized assessed value per student in Ontario. The distribution is notable for its "outliers," numbers that are very different from most values. There are about a dozen out of 170 school boards that are unusual; a half-dozen have practically no assessment and a half dozen have extremely high assessments. As it turns out, most of the latter are in major metropolitan areas, especially Ottawa and Metropolitan Toronto.

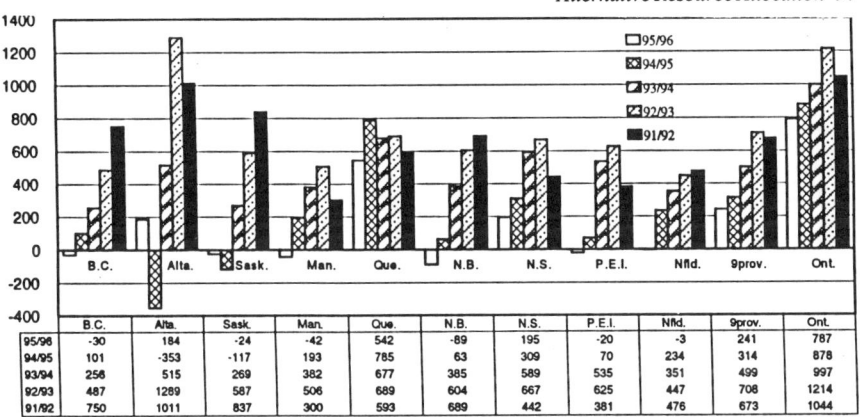

	B.C.	Alta.	Sask.	Man.	Que.	N.B.	N.S.	P.E.I.	Nfld.	9prov.	Ont.
95/96	-30	184	-24	-42	542	-89	195	-20	-3	241	787
94/95	101	-353	-117	193	785	63	309	70	234	314	878
93/94	256	515	269	382	677	385	589	535	351	499	997
92/93	487	1289	587	506	689	604	667	625	447	708	1214
91/92	750	1011	837	300	593	689	442	381	476	673	1044

Provincial Deficit/Capita
(negative = surplus)
($/person)

Source: Lawton, Ryall & Menzies, 1996

consolidated deficit/capital (including operating and capital items), from TD Department of Economic Research, Report on Provincial Government Finances, Aug/94 & Aug/95
prov9 weighted average based on provincial 94/95 populations

Figure 3: Consolidated Deficit/Surplus Per Capita (Negative = Surplus)

EAV/P is used as an index of a school board's ability to pay for education since local funding is derived, in Ontario, from the property tax on real property. It is a logical connection, but one which is flawed. The problem is that people and businesses do not pay their taxes out of wealth that is locked into real estate that is used, in the case of families, as homes, or, in the case of businesses, to earn income. That is, the value of property is not a good estimate of the ability of on individual or business to pay a tax. In one sense, this is an argument against the property tax, as it is currently implemented; that is, based on market value assessments of real estate. Why, if we want to have a wealth tax, why do we not tax other forms of wealth – stocks, bonds, art collections, etc.? Or, if we wish to tax real property, why do we not tax on its ability to earn income rather than as a store of locked-in wealth. Even with stocks and bonds, increases in value are taxed only as capital gains when they are sold. Why should the treatment of real estate be different?

The use of market value assessment was a "solution" to several problems perceived by economists and city planners in the 1950s and 1960s. They decreed the "misallocation" of land and "encouragement" of speculation that occurred when property was taxed according to its ability to earn income or the burden that servicing the property placed on local government. The latter two approaches effectively treat the property tax as a tax on income or as a user fee on benefits gained by the owner. Critics saw speculators holding vacant land, waiting for capital gains, and residential property near high density centres whose "best use" was for development. Higher property taxes, reflecting the properties' market value, would force the development of these lands sooner, and allow government to capture part of the gain in value on an annual basis. These policy advisors did not anticipate an inflationary period during which baby boomers would crowd the property market, or the potential depopulation of central cities as property taxes rose.

At the same time provinces were moving to market value assessment of real property, the federal government dropped inheritance taxes, which have been the most traditional tax on wealth, leaving that area to the provinces. However, no province dared to enact an inheritance tax for fear older individuals would move wealth out of the province.

The underlying problem with the use of the property tax based on equalized assessed value is also evident by comparing the value of single family residences with household income, as in Figures 4 and 5. Although these data are for the 1980 census, the current distributions would be quite similar. It is evident from these figures that the market value of a family's home is a poor measure of its members' ability to pay taxes. Although persons living in dense urban areas may own property that is of much higher in value than do those in smaller centres or rural areas, urban dwellers do not have a substantially greater ability to pay: their incomes, on average, are little or no higher. The popular view is that residents of big centres benefit greatly from the concentration of valuable commercially property in their municipalities. Indeed, this view prompted the Ontario Liberal government of David Peterson to enact the "corporate concentration tax," which was in essence a provincial property tax on Metro Toronto. While urban residents do gain services from taxes on commercial property, the fact is that the high values placed on their residential properties mean that, in order to purchase the same level of public service, they actually pay higher taxes than do those in outlying areas with lower assessed value.

A measure of the cost of providing local services is referred to as their "tax price." It is defined as the amount of tax a resident must pay to purchase a dollar's worth of a service, such as education. Residents of Metro Toronto have a tax price for education that is above that for the rest of the province (Lawton, 1985).

When a province decides to make grants to school boards, it must determine both the level of need in the schools and the elector's level of ability to pay. Both require judgments as to equity, one to students and one to taxpayers. But provincial governments should consider not just social justice, but also economic justice; i.e., allowing individuals and communities to enjoy the fruits of their labors. One of the greatest public policy errors of the post-war period was to underestimate the effects of transfer payments on the behavior of both individuals and organizations. When grants are given to provinces, school boards, hospitals, or other agencies, the prices of their services to the public are lowered, and lower prices stimulate demand. Along the way, the employees of service organizations benefit in terms of more, higher paying jobs. The result is a demand for more service from a public that thinks it can afford it, although it could not. The increasing levels of educational expenditures charted by Gendron reflect this growth in demand. If citizens had to pay the full cost up-front, they would have been more temperate in their demands and less generous in allowing trustees and officials to increase the number and remuneration of educators and other public servants.

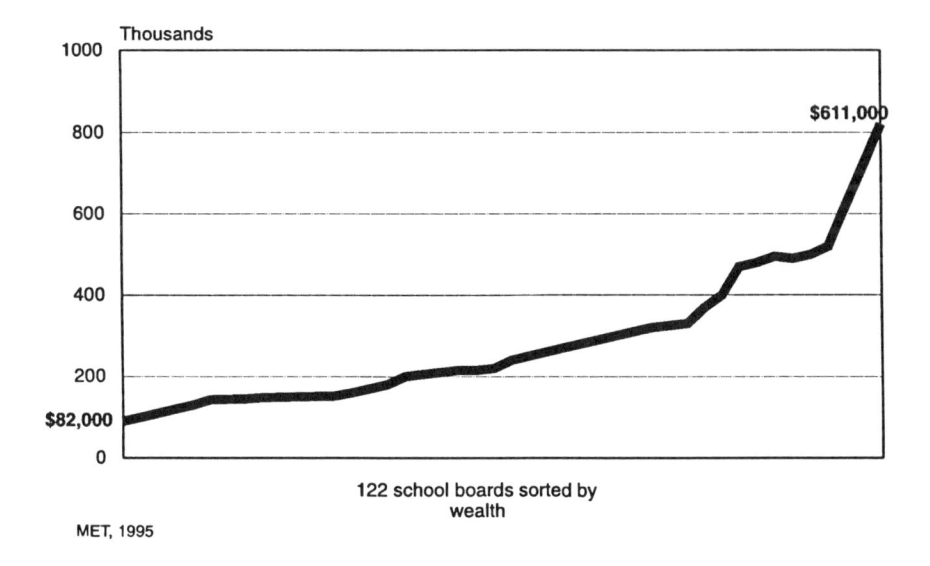

[Figure: Line chart showing assessment wealth rising from $82,000 to $611,000 across 122 school boards sorted by wealth. Source: MET, 1995]

Figure 5: Assessment Wealth Comparison (1993 per student equalized assessment by board)

Another pernicious effect of subsidies is the creation of a dual economy in geographic areas that receive inordinate subsidies. Provincially, the Atlantic provinces exhibit this effect. Jobs funded, at least in part, by transfer payments from the federal government, including teachers, are the best paid and most stable. Such positions are sought as sinecures. A secondary effect, caused by their lack of connection to the "real economy," is that educators fail to appreciate the true value of their efforts in terms of the local private-sector wage rates, or the competitive skills their charges will need in order to survive in the real economy. This phenomenon also occurs in rural and smaller centres across the country, where teachers are the elite, with the largest homes, most secure and generous pensions, and most frequent holidayer in Florida. Also implicated in the operation of this false economy are the teachers' unions that have, as Gendron notes, been able to ensure a rigid salary system that protects the employment income of the majority of their members (see figure 7).

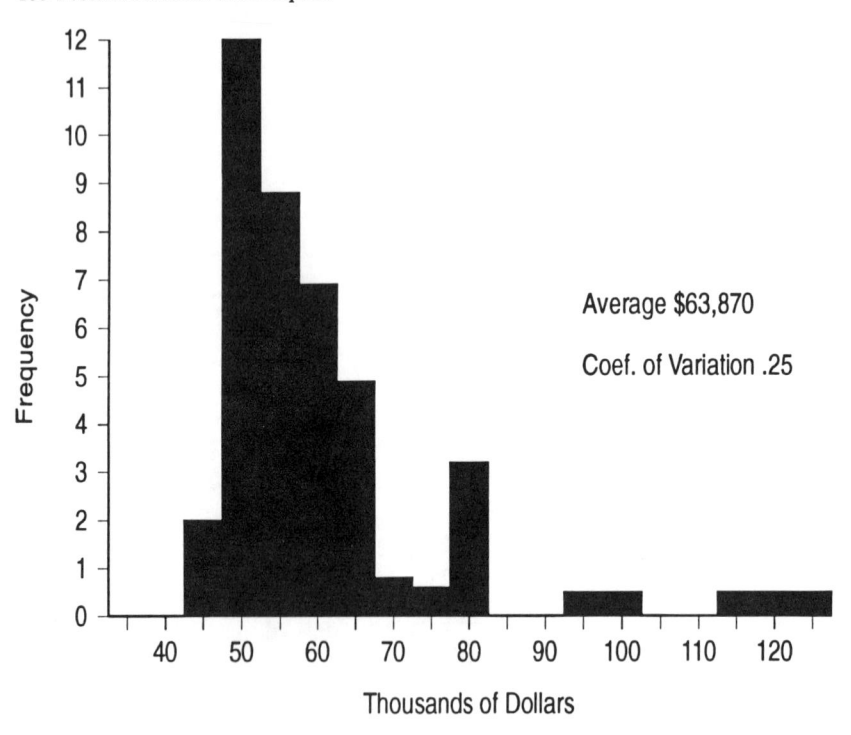

Figure 6: Average Value of Dwellings in Southern Ontario Counties and Cities

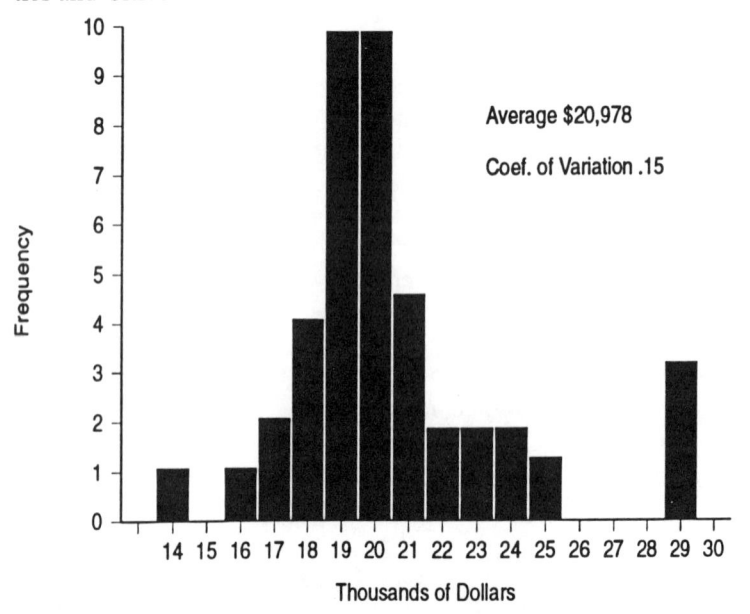

Figure 7: Average Household Income in Ontario Counties and Cities

An alternative system of funding education is reflected in the United States. Schemes used in most states, though superficially similar to those in many Canadian provinces, have avoided the worst extremes evident here. With weaker teachers' associations and bargaining at the local level, American teachers' salaries exhibit far more variation within a state than do their Canadian counterparts. A recent report indicated that in major urban centres U.S. teachers typically enjoyed salaries 10% above their state norms; in rural areas, with low costs of living, salaries were typically 15% below average. In contrast, a study of costs of educational inputs in Ontario (Lawton, et al., 1988) found modest variation between rural and urban. In addition to having expenditures or tax rates in order to control costs (Gold, et al., 1995). How long this situation in the U.S. will continue is uncertain, however, since numerous court cases are underway in which plaintiffs argue that education is a state responsibility which demands more uniform allocation policies, like those already in effect in Canadian provinces.

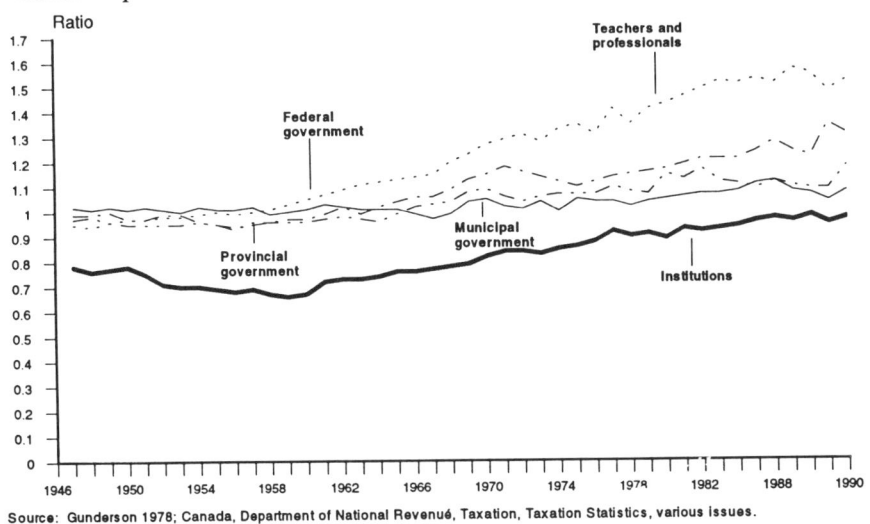

Figure 8: Ratios of Public to Private Sector Wages, 1946-90

The trend in Canada to "solve" the "equity" problem has been to move toward full provincial funding. Most recent to take this action is Alberta, as noted above, which took the occasion to begin a reallocation of all funds available to education, including what had been the local property tax. British Columbia and Newfoundland had adopted full provincial funding several years earlier. Currently, four provinces, Prince Edward Island and New Brunswick being the other two, have full provincial funding of education. Different allocation practices are used in each case. Newfoundland, for example, allocates the number of teaching positions to a school board on the basis of school size, allows the school district to hire the teachers, but then pays the teachers directly from the treasurer's office. British Columbia uses a complex "fiscal framework" that includes input costs and characteristics of programs to determine the grant, and therefore expenditure, levels. The latter province is also assuming the responsibility to bargain salaries. Provincial authority and teachers' unions power will be the guides in these provinces.

While this trend toward centralized funding has the merit of controlling costs (so long as the provincial government remains strong in the face of the challenge, say, of a province-wide strike) and achieving "equity" by whatever standard is set in the formula and practices adopted, it totally severs any connection between the local educational system and the local economy. The notion of "economic justice" on an intra-provincial basis goes by the wayside. Persons in areas of low wealth and low cost will have teachers paid more than the local economy could justify, while those higher cost areas may find it difficult to attract teachers. It would be possible to negotiate regional differentiation in pay, but this is only practicable if a few areas exhibit striking needs, such as remote areas in the north. Otherwise, uniformity will prevail.

Provincial direction of this type is deleterious both financially and educationally since it institutionalizes the dual economy – one government and one private – at the local level. In the short run, this provincialization may continue to mean teachers will be paid more highly than other local residents in rural areas and smaller centres. If the local economy thrives, however, they may be left behind since provinces will be unable to increase their expenditures until provincial debts are reduced.

This argument for economic justice may sound penurious, but it is meant to encourage the balanced development of individuals and communities. Judicious investment in a basic education for those who cannot otherwise afford it is one thing, but arguing that all should enjoy the educational consumption of facilities with dedicated music rooms, rubberized tracks, and the like is quite another. If a community has not earned these accoutrement, or its citizens do not wish to sacrifice their own hard-earned money to purchase them, then it does not deserve them. Instead of a sense of relative deprivation which motivates them to fight with others over who is to benefit most from provincial largess, they will experience a degree genuine deprivation and be motivated, as many others have in the past, to succeed for themselves, their children, and their community.

Refining Equity to Encourage Efficiency and Adaptability

Communities are not nearly so unequal in their ability to pay for public services as the use of data on equalized assessed value per student suggests. A redesigned school finance system could better capture local ability in several ways, without turning to full provincial control. First, one could rebate part of the income tax and sales tax collected from residents of a jurisdiction to their school board to increase its "local revenue." This process is equivalent to that used by the federal government for funding postsecondary education and health by "returning tax points" to the provinces. It is a way of tagging money and saying, "This is your money, not the province's."

Second, property assessment could be reformed by taxing land and improvements separately, with the property tax based only on the value of the improvements. What differs between densely populated areas and outlying areas is not so much the value of the structures as the value of the land. The taxing of land could be restricted to land transfer taxes. Other proposals have been made that would have a similar effect.

Third, a complementary "workplace" income tax might be set to recognize the needs of communities in which people work rather then live. In this way, those who live in one city but work in another would contribute directly to the support of services in these jurisdictions.

Finally, a more equitable corporate income tax could be used that would relate to a corporation's profits rather than to the value of its fixed assets; as a result, commercial and industrial rates for educational and municipal services could be reduced.

In provinces with shared financing arrangements, such as Manitoba and Ontario, the net result of these reforms would be less variation in revenue among school boards even before provincial grants were considered. Instead of having political decisions made by those remote from the scene, a natural distribution of funds would occur which could be supplemented with provincial grants in cases where there was evident need.

In particular, equalization grants could be given to those whose ability to pay (as measured by income from property tax, income tax rebated, and sales tax rebated) was ranked in the lowest 25%. Parsimony, not penury, would rule.

The approach to funding would be a far more dynamic and responsive system than that which we have at present in any Canadian province, especially those that have mistakenly centralized funding in the belief that they are ensuring equity and efficiency. With the proposed system, economic growth in a community would immediately translate into a more expansive educational system or lower taxes, according to the values of the community. Provincial treasuries and politicians would have a system that required less tending, and teachers in communities would know that their own interests were tied to the business and commercial interests of their cities, towns, villages, and farms. Investments in education would be made wisely, since the negative effects of excessive taxation would be evident. Conversely, those in industry, commerce, and public service would see the value of contributing to a strong educational system in their community.

References

Canadian Centre for Policy Alternatives (1995). *The 1995 alternative federal budget.* Ottawa, ON: The Centre.

Treff, Karin & Cook Ted (1995). *Finances of the nation.* Toronto, ON: Canadian Tax Foundation.

Gendron, François (1994). "Does Canada invest enough in education? An insight into the cost structure of education in Canada," *Education Quarterly Review.* Statistics Canada – Cat. No. 81-003 Vol. No. 4: 10-24.

Gold, Steven D., Smith, David M. & Lawton, Stephen B. (1995). *Public school finance programs of the United States and Canada, 1993-94.* Albany, NY: American Education Finance Association and the Centre for the Study of the States.

Government of Canada (1995) *Budget belief.* Ottawa, ON: Ministry of Finance.

Lankford, Hamilton & Wycoff, James (1995). "Where has the money gone? An analysis of school district spending in New York. *Educational Evaluation and Policy Analysis, Summer, Vol.17, No. 2*: 195-218.

Lawton, Stephen B. (1985). "Economic models explaining school board expenditure," *Journal of Education Finance, Vol. 11, No. 2*: 236-257.

Lawton, Stephen B. (June 1993). "Thoughts for the future of education finance in Canada." CTF Seminar on The Impact of Federal Economic Policies on Public Education and Teachers, June 20-22, 1993. Ottawa, ON: The Canadian Teachers' Federation. Photocopy of edited transcription.

Lawton, Stephen B., James, Gordon, Paquette, Jerry & Tzalalis, Theodore (1988). *Cost of education index for Ontario,.* Toronto, ON: Ministry of Education.

Ministry of Education and Training (1994). *Education funding in Ontario – A description of the funding model.* Toronto, ON: MET.

Perry, David B. (1995). "Provincial budget roundup," *Canadian Tax Journal, Vol. 43, No. 3:* 660-695.

Treff, Karin (1992). "Education financing in Canada," *Canadian Tax Journal, Vol.40, No. 2*: 501-518.

8

Eking Out the Last Dollars: Non-traditional Funding for Education

V. Hajnal & K. Walker

Try asking the general public about the funding of K-12 education. Business leaders frequently complain that schools cost too much. Parents protest about the added costs of school supplies and extras, such as trips. Home owners are concerned about the property taxes which go to support the education system. And everyone complains about income tax and sales tax. While the Gallup polls and other surveys clearly indicate that many parents and non-parents (70% in 1996) would be prepared to contribute more to the cost of education (CTF, 1996), parents from specific localities may be opposed to property tax increases. Fearing reprisals from a local electorate, boards of education are apprehensive about raising property taxes. Consequently it is left to the school community to eke out the last dollars in support of education.

While this chapter addresses non-traditional funding in K-12 education, the first section describes traditional funding sources in Canada. The second section provides a typology of fund raising in schools and school divisions. The third section descerbers the experiences of Saskatchewan educators with non-traditional funding. The final section discusses the implications.

Traditional Funding

Throughout Canada the funding of K-12 education has remained, in the most part, the responsibility of the provinces. The federal government has direct responsibility for children of armed forces personnel on military bases, of Native and Inuit Peoples and people who live in the non-provincial parts of Canada (Yukon, Nunavut and Denedeh) as well as for second official language immersion instruction.

School boards and the school jurisdictions, which have been the predominant governance structure for schools in Canada, have been the conduit for provincial funding for K-12 education. The provinces support K-12 education through grants to school boards. On a provincial average, this level of support can range from 40% to 100%. Where not prohibited, school jurisdictions raise additional funds from local property taxes. However, a trend toward more centralized educational funding is clear with more provinces abolishing the right of school boards to levy property taxes.

While grants and property taxes produce over 95% of the revenues for school boards, a small percentage of funds (less than 5%) come from other sources such as tuition fees and sale of buildings or capital assets.

During the 1990s, as national and provincial governments attended to decreasing their deficits and controlling the debt, downward pressures have been placed on education spending. For example, across Canada in 1996-97, per student spending was expected to decline by 1.2% (CTF, 1997). Perceiving ever-increasing needs and receiving less funds at the school level, administrators, teachers, parents, and students have become fund raisers.

Non-traditional Funding

Non-traditional funds may be collected at the school and/or the school system level and include voluntary contributions as well as fees. Voluntary contributions are perceived to be gifts. Brown (1993, p. 192) indicates volunteer funding is increasing even though these receipts will form a very small portion of the overall K-12 education budget. However, they do form a significant portion of the discretionary budget of a school.

Describing fund-raising by the purpose it supports provides one way to categorize funds. Funds can be raised for special, general or altruistic purposes. Special purpose funds are identified as fees, collected for a particular school purpose and spent on that purpose. These fees include special levies for supplies, books, field trips, and similar activities.

General purpose funds have increased significantly during the last decade. Funds are collected for use within the school, but they are not levies. Nouraddin (1995) provided a typology for their classification. Type 1 involves selling commercial goods and services such as gift wrap, boxed cookies, magazine subscriptions, dried fruit, and citrus fruit. Type II includes the selling of non-commercial goods and services such as baked goods, crafts, garage sales, and car washes. Type III concerns entering into private agreements for cash, in-kind donations, scholarships, and other gifts. Although businesses are often involved, sponsorship is the operative word. Receiving a time clock for gym with a company logo would be a Type III transaction. Type IV arrangements concern ongoing enterprise activities, including vending machines, cafeteria operations and renting school facilities. These arrangements are business transactions with access to markets being sold and are often labelled concessions.

Schools also help raise money for specific purposes for other groups. This arrangement implies and altruistic purpose. Children raise money for the United Way, UNICEF, other charities and occasional needs in the community, such as after a fire or flood.

Integrating these classifications provides the conceptualization presented in Figure 1. Fund-raising is typified the organizational level, the purpose and the arrangements. This table provides a reference point for those involved with fund-raising in schools to examine the extent of their involvement and determine the policy needs for their organization.

	Level of the Decision-making in the Organization	
Purpose	School	School Division
Special	Fees collected for special purpose e.g. books, field trips, supplies. They cannot be diverted to support other needs.	This column repeats the information in the previous column.
General	Funds are collected to support the school in general and can be used for any purpose.	
Arrangements	Type 1: selling commercial goods and services Type 2: selling non-commercial goods and services	
	Type 3: sponsorship to build a company or individuals goodwill Type 4: on-going enterprise activities	
Altruistic	Funds are collected for charities or other needy individuals or groups	

Figure 1: Fund-Raising in an Educational Setting: A Typology Based on Organizational Level, Purpose, and Arrangment

Non-traditional Funding in Saskatchewan Schools

The Need

In the 1990s Saskatchewan school boards experienced decreases in funding to K-12 education, while experiencing increasing demands. As a result of these pressures, Hanjal (1995) conducted a study in 1994 to examine how school boards were coping. School divisions were forced to tighten their belts, absorbing most of the increased costs and decreased revenues, and then to reduce the programs and services available to students. As well, boards turned to entrepreneurial ways to increase the funds they received. Schools were also hit with reductions in their budget allocations. This was particularly painful because Saskatchewan Education (provincial ministry responsible for K-12 education) had instigated a move toward resource-based learning and funds were required to purchase the necessary resources.

The Extent

The extent of the fund-raising, the practices and concerns were described with reference to a formal study conducted by Walker and Langlois (1996) and two informal interviews with principals.

Informal Interviews

Describing their approach to fund-raising and where they spent these funds, the two administrators painted interested pictures of their activities. George acknowledged that his school, in a rural jurisdiction, did not lack for any resources. "I can get whatever I want for my school." He had been in the school for several years, had the support of parents, and raised funds on an on-going bases. George acknowledged that his superintendent was not clear about the school's fund-raising activities and George's accountability for the funds appeared marginal.

Linda, the second administrator, had a well-ordered cohesion to the approach in her school. The parent advisory council played a major role in the fund-raising. If funds were required for some purpose, the proposal went to the parent advisory council and it was this group that gave the approval or suggested a reduced amount for the activity. The bulk of the funds were obtained from working at bingos, with parents, administrators, and teachers contributing their time to this effort. They had one additional major sale a year of dried fruit, Christmas wrap, or other commodity, generally before Christmas. They also had minor events such as hot-dog sales. With a population of 135 students, these activities raised $15 000 annually. The funds were used for field trips, library materials, gym equipment and curricular needs. Linda explained, "If we wanted a sponge ball for 31 students in a classroom, we could have that many and they didn't have to share." The accountability was evident in her conversation, but she acknowledged that the superintendent would not have been enamored with all the expenditures.

Questionnaire

In 1995 using surveys, Walker and Langlois examined non-traditional funding for K-12 education in Saskatchewan. Random samples of 200 school-based administrators and 150 central office personnel which included superintendents, secretary-treasurers, and Board chairpersons were selected for the study. The response rate for school-based administrators was 66% and 52% for the central office personnel. Thirty-two percent of respondents were from divisions with a budget less than $6 million, 46% had a budget between $6-10 million and 22% had operating budgets greater than $10 million.

Fund-raising activities at the school level were reported by 97% of the school administrators surveyed. At the division level, fund-raising activities were reported by 64% of division level respondents. Seventy-six percent of school administrators and central office personnel believed that parents encouraged fund-raising. The most frequently selected criticisms included saturation and overkill, interference with instruction, accountability, double taxation, safety and liability. Some educational value was attributed to fund-raising-in the realm of school spirit, responsibility, pride, organizational skills, awareness of the less fortunate, school-community cooperation.

Several agencies asked school divisions and schools to raise funds for charities, such as UNICEF, Telemiracle, Heart and Stroke Foundation, United Way and others.

The programs and activities that were financed through fund raising at the school level included Student Council activities, yearbook, graduation program, field trips, and athletics including uniforms and referees. Activities which were most frequently used for fund-raising included sales within the school such as pizza, sales within the community such as cookies, commission from photo and book fairs, student fees for specific purposes, national or provincial programs (such as poppy sales), and donations from school-related agencies.

Policy considerations.

Less than 60% of respondents affirmed that their school divisions had policies in place that dealt explicitly with school fund-raising. Approximately half of the respondents suggested that their school division did not have specific policy concerning the handling of money generated by school fund-raising.

Respondents foresaw an ever-increasing need for fund-raising as there was a greater reduction in funding provided to and from the division level "Fund-raising will be needed to finance things other than traditional activities like sports" said one respondent. "It will be needed for computers, books, and field trips."

Equity of educational opportunity was a policy issue for some respondents. Concerns that belonged to this category were: making have and have-not jurisdictions, unequal resources for schools translated into unequal education among students; how is money divided among the student population; and should school funds be collected at the school level or pooled at the division level and distributed to all schools through a central budget. Only 13% of the comments regarding policy issues raised from fund-raising were directly attributed to equity concerns.

Implications for Schools and School Boards

Funding school programs and activities through non-traditional sources is increasing. Millions of dollars are being collected almost exclusively at the school level in a variety of ways including sales, raffles, bingos, "A-thons," car washes, carnivals, fun nights, advertising, partnerships, and so on. What was in the not too distant past the occasional or special initiative in schools is now common place.

Much of this fund-raising activity is occurring on an ad hoc basis with organizers lacking knowledge of school division policies to govern fund-raising. For the most part, school-based administrators are left to their own devices in finding ways to supplement traditional funding sources to finance programs and activities.

As well, non-traditional funding sources are being used to finance programs that, at one time, were fully funded through taxation. School division personnel view the scope and purpose of fund-raising activities to be narrower than the actual experience reported by school-based administrators. School division personnel viewed fund-raising activities to be more support of co-curricular programs such as graduations, yearbooks, and drama nights and seemed less aware or willing to acknowledge that non-traditional funding was being used increasingly to support instructional programs.

Positive outcomes from fund-raising activities, including improved school spirit, student understanding of goals, better school-community cooperation and helping worthwhile causes have merit, but there are many concerns with the fund-raising practices. These concerns included, among others, overkill and saturation in the community, inadequate accountability and accounting at the school level, interference with instruction, and double taxation. A tension between the desire to provide more opportunities for students or helping worthwhile causes, on the one hand, and the need to engage in fund-raising, on the other hand, appears to exist. School-based administrators were very mindful of community expectations and attempted to guide their schools accordingly. However, without policy direction, it can be expected that, as the number of activities increases, the potential for conflict within the school community and the larger community will also increase.

Given these trends, boards of education should consider the development of policies and guidelines to assist school-based personnel in determining the scope and nature of non-traditional funding activities within the school division. School-based personnel are entitled to know school system expectations and limitations pertaining to fund-raising programs. For example, does the board approve monopolistic practices such as exclusive rights to sell particular products in exchange for free service or equipment? Does the board encourage schools to support charitable organizations? Does the board permit the selling of products in direct competition with local merchants who pay taxes in support of the school? In most cases, these are political and ethical decisions now being made by administrators seeking funding sources for worthwhile school functions.

In addition to knowing the parameters within which they can raise funds in support of school functions, school-based administrators must also be provided with the necessary tools to manage funds appropriately. Respondents in the Saskatchewan survey identified accounting and accountability as a serious concern – likely with cause. Issues related to safekeeping of funds, spending in accordance with stated objectives, financial accountability to the community, reporting of activities to school division authorities, and sound purchasing practices should be addressed within a policy context.

As the scope and nature of fund-raising activities expands, school division administrators can expect to be called upon more frequently to resolve conflicts among competing interests. Conflicts will take different forms including opposition to fund-raising for school purposes in principle, objection to specific activities, concern about competition with local businesses, inappropriate use of funds, and inadequate reporting. Administrators will be expected to deal with the fund-raising industry which is also expanding as they find willing clients. They will also be asked with increasing frequency to permit the administrators within their divisions to participate in national and provincial fund-raising programs. These administrators should be responding with a policy framework rather than responding solely on their personal beliefs and particular values.

Educators should also be concerned about the student involvement in these activities. What lessons are learned when the decision is made to undertake a particular fund-raising program? Is time spent fund-raising a sound educational practice or does it detract from the primary mission of the school? Is it clear that there are both benefits and costs for students engaged in these activities. As it pertains to students, it would seem the issue is not so much whether or not fund-raising is to be done but whether it is managed in an appropriate manner.

Finally, as fund-raising activities increase to supplement tax-based funds, the relationship between the school, on the one hand, and the parents and community, on the other, may be altered in a significant way. Schools can expect increased resistance to their initiatives for a variety of reasons. For example, at what point does support for school programs became unfair competition for the local business paying school taxes? Does the selling of raffle tickets offend the values of some families? Should the tax supported school complete for funds with other community groups, not tax funded, providing services on a volunteer basis? Will fund-raising lead to tax resistance?

Fund-raising in support of school programs and activities has been increasing, partly in response to funding reductions and partly to support an ever widening range of opportunities available to pupils. It is unrealistic to expect that fund-raising activities will not expand in the future. The issues to be confronted deal with the appropriate management of these activities to ensure that community support for schools will continue.

References

Brown, D.J. (1994, June). What is school enterprise? Paper presented at the annual meeting of the Canadian Society for the Study of Education in Calgary.

Canadian Teachers' Federation (1996, November/December). Economic Service Notes, #1996-10 Ottawa, ON: CTF Canadian Teachers' Federation (1997, February). Economic Service Notes, #1997-2. Ottawa, ON: CTF.

Hajnal, V.J.(1995). Public school finance in Saskatchewan: An Introspection. Saskatchewan School Trustees Association Research Centre Report #95-01. Regina, SK: SSTA.

Lawton, S.B. (1996). *Financing Canadian education*. Toronto, ON: Canadian Education Association.

Nouraddin, A. (1995). Private resources for public education. Unpublished doctoral dissertation, University of Toronto, Ontario.

Walker, K. & Langois, H. (1996). Alternative and non-traditional funding for K-12 education in Saskatchewan, Saskatchewan School Trustees Association Research Centre Report #96-14. Regina, SK: SSTA.

Walker, K. (1996). "A blushing romance: Framework for an ethical exposition of a relationship between educational and commercial interests," *McGill Journal of Education, 31(3)*. 275-296.

9

Chaperonic Reflections on the Relations Between Business and Education Sectors

Keith Walker and Brent Kay

A Blushing Romance

All signs point to the fact that business-education arrangements are increasing at a nimble pace and that, in some instances, neither party is quite sure about the propriety of the underlying terms and consequences implicit in such relations. On the one hand, they seem to like each other's company and the other, they frequently express bewilderment towards the intentions and levels or kinds of interests of the other. Onlookers of the courtship rituals have had much to laud or lament about the increasing frequency, expanding nature, and intensification of this romance. Some commentators are encouraging; while others warn of the inevitability of exploitation or perils of "dining with the devil." To say the least, views within the education arena are diverse.

The antagonism to such relations was typified in a recent newspaper heading that read, "School Board Sells Out to its Students in Deal with Pepsi." Another headline felicitates a "Computers for Schools Offer by National Food Chain" by criticizing two systems for rejecting a company's offer to help prepare children. A third press release says "School Board Signs Partnership Agreements with Twenty Private Sector Companies." The agreement is heralded for providing numerous projects, all aimed to benefit students through the use of explicit learning outcomes.

If one adds to these examples the national print and television magazine coverage of violence in schools, claims of poor academic performances compared to students from other countries, the high drop out rates, criticism of youth lifestyles, literacy levels and work ethics of high school graduates, and the plethora of other sharp indictments aimed at assessing the current state of North American education systems, then the magnitude of the debate surrounding business-education relations is better understood. We read of the business attempts, some new and some long-standing, to establish Charter schools, to privatize Kindergartens, to establish company schools. and to have business consortiums manage entire school systems; however, often these initiatives are met with skepticism by both public and academic counterparts. Business advice-givers have cogently told educators how to market their schools, how to operate using private sector "quality" models, and how to enhance consumer choice through the use of school league scores to determine a schools fitness and viability. Media reports and commentaries such as these bombard with their mixed reviews of the state of education and particularly its relations with the private sector.

Social commentators provide varied explanations for the apparent increase in attention directed by the media, courts, government offices, town halls, and coffee rows to the plight and potential of North American educational institutions. Alarmist public analyses has declared a wide range of views with respect to the "risk," importance, and impotency that follows for nations who are unwilling to smarten up their education systems. The phenomenon of high profile and quickly conceived compacts between public and private sector interests and, particularly, between business and education, prompts us to ask about the nature, legitimacy, and the ethical status of these various romances. This chapter aims to provide a description of some existing relations between business and education because we think that this phenomena is inevitably going to grow and, true to past experience, will result in both enormous benefit and significant regret for education sector. We would suggest that if it can be agreed that business-education relations are in a state of rapid expansion, then we must ensure ethical guidelines are in place to guide the creation of mutually beneficial arrangements in the future. Furthermore, that careful ethical scrutiny of business and education relations will prevent the loss of well-conceived opportunities for legitimate philanthropic and reciprocal relations and at the same time provide mechanisms for avoidance of exploitive and potentially scandalous relations.

Not a New Romance: But a Rekindled One

In Canada, as with some American and European countries, social programs and services such as health, social welfare, and education have been strongly supported by government funding for over fifty years. However, since the 1980s, governments have drastically reduced contributions to these dependent services and agencies. Individual and corporate philanthropy has been challenged over the last decade to fill the void and, in the case of education, to help meet the increased fiscal demands of education systems. This recent response to the debt-reducing cutbacks in the public sector has been met with a tremendous response from the private sector, who have made inestimable contributions to education in the last number of years.

Timpane (1988) comments on the "unprecedented array of state legislative and policy-making activity" that has flooded these countries and made education "one of the highest items on everyone's agenda in the development of national economic health" (p. 228). From his ten-year-old and American perspective, he says that the participation of the business community in education "has developed so widely and deeply that now it is almost assumed" (p. 228). Non-traditional supports to educational services have become topics of dialog and consternation to school boards and educational professionals. Education and business represent two significant sector forces that mould the social culture. Their common interests may be examined by considering their zone of interaction in the context of society.

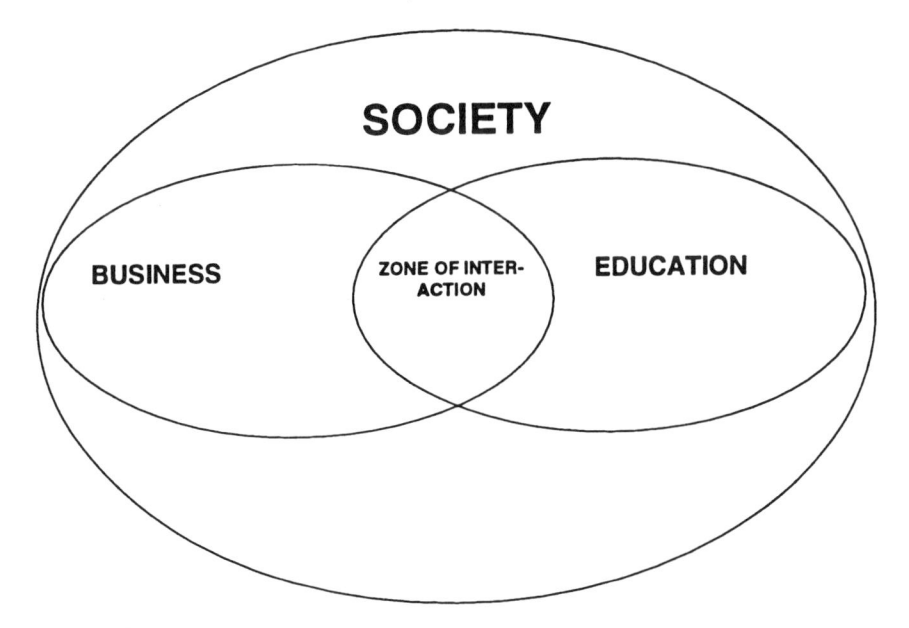

Figure 1: Business-Education Relations: Zone of Interaction

In the latter 20th century, prior to the information explosion, the zone of interaction between business and education was limited to the transition from school to the workforce. Since the information explosion, a technocratic society has emerged that has relied on experts to determine the common good for society (Westrum, 1991). The impact of our technocratic society on business-education relations has been two-fold. First, the development of a society that is heavily dependent on technology has prompted the business community to place increased demands on education to produce more qualified workers. Second, the rising costs of education have provoked widespread criticism over the rate of return this financial investment is providing (Parnes, 1984; Berg, 1971) and, as a result, increased resource competition from other social services such as welfare and health care has prospered (Lawton, 1987).

Business demands on education to produce more qualified workers and increased competition for financial resources have facilitated a rapid expansion of the zone of interaction. Young (1986) reported that "more and more business corporations are becoming dissatisfied with the quality of education and are becoming involved. At times they help out with resources, at other times they set up alternatives to the public and private schools" (p. 14). Education also welcomes a greater interaction with business. For example, in 1984 the Alberta Teachers' Association referred to the business community as a "precious teaching resource" (p. 2) and many Canadian provinces have become actively involved in seeking corporate sponsorship. Such developments suggest that the education and business sectors have actively sought each other's company; however, their intensions and interests appear to stem from divergent and perhaps incommensurable perspectives.

Mix of Intentions and Interests?

While relationships may succeed despite of the fact or perception that partners are unequally yoked, the nature of the intentions and interests of those in relations should not be assumed. What are the intentions and interests of business and what about those in the education sector? There are some fundamental differences between business and education. For example, it may be said of education that one of its primary goals is to prepare our youth to be productive members of society. In recent years, this goal has been expanded due to the implementation of compulsory attendance legislation by the Canadian provinces require children to remain in school a certain age (typically 16). Kay (1994) indicated that in 1970, 64 percent of 17-year-olds and 42 percent 18-year-olds were enrolled in school. By 1990, these figures had increased to 80 percent and 55 percent, respectively. The age of educational dependence has been expanded to include virtually all children older than 6 and up to 17, inclusive, and over half of those 18 years of age.

Upon graduation, students enter a period of transition where they apply the knowledge, gained during formative years, to the work-a-day world. The transition phase from education to work is a most challenging period: the student life ceases and the high demands of the work-world become evident. During this period, the individual enters a new environment, where educational interests and intentions are often replaced with those of the commercial sector. While the primary goals of education often are related to the development of well-rounded and flourishing members of society, the primary goals of business are usually associated with making profit for shareholders.

Educators are by no means unanimous with respect to their educational values and their philosophic views. Some say schools ought to allow children to grow as expressive, tolerant, and harmonious individuals. Others say education prepares children as citizens and workers while others claim that the cultivation of the intellect, aesthetic, and social senses is what education is all about. To some, the prime purpose of education is to develop good character and to transmit cultural values, from generation to generation. Others, feel the primary purpose of education is to challenge every child to the excellences afforded by their unique limits, abilities, and interests; egalitarian educators see education as focused on the harmonious development of all children, in an equal manner.

On reflection, schools are often expected to demonstrate values such as justice, integrity, equity, full participation, inclusion, and fairness (Calabrese, 1990). Business interests are usually seen as having commercial interests and to hold profit as a central goal, although this perception is sometimes debated.

Increasing societal concern about corporate ethics and about the assumption of social responsibility by commercial institutions are commonly expressed (Lewis, 1990). Corporations in North America have a long history of contributing to socially worthwhile causes, including education (Carroll, 1989; Sturdivant and Vernon-Wortzel, 1990), but this focus does not imply a lack of concern for other values.

The business and education communities have different concerns that must be addressed to promote mutually beneficial relationships in the future. For example, the business community supports a closer relationship with education because they consider the primary goal of education to be, "the development of the productive members of society – a large part of which is spent in the workforce" (Young, 1986, p. 14). In addition, business deems corporate involvement in education as necessary because, "the gap between what is needed in the contemporary information society workplace and the educational attainment of school graduates is enormous" (Young, 1986, p. 15). Bakalis (1987) identifies yet another corporate interest by stating that "business dialogue may filled with discussions of bottom-line, increased productivity, competition, and accountability, but these concepts are simply not part of teachers' standard educational vocabulary or dialogue" (p. 48). And Wright (1989) adds, "there is reason why schools cannot be run like businesses, achieving objectives of the organization as efficiently as possible while keeping a sharp focus on the bottom line. The problem is that most teachers, principals, and superintendents do not possess business management skills and, as a result, our education systems suffer" (p. 18).

In response to these imputations, education retorts that it needs to maintain its own agenda. Reich (1984) depicts American business' "much trumpeted support for education as a smoke screen that obscures a more profound corporate withdrawal from the public education sector" (in Weisman, 1991, p. 10). Reich suggested that business has become an influential advocate of school reform, it has worked to acquire subsidies and tax breaks from all levels of government. In the light of mixed motivations, educational leaders may feel any proposed business-education engagements ought to be reviewed.

In summary, both education and business sectors have unique concerns regarding the potential for future arrangements with each other. Business people view education as a necessary development tool for tommorrow's economic future but are often critical of the educator's abilities to create systems capable meeting these demands. Second, educators remain skeptical of increased business involvement. There exists a need to be reflective in the management of these relationships and to ensure that mutually beneficial arrangements are established.

The rapid increase in the zone of interaction between business and education has resulted in a situation where many educators and business people are merely operating in response to opportunities and have not thought through their respective governing values. We predict that the zone of interaction will expand in the future. Just as it has been said that technology has developed in ways that far exceeded the social-ethical acumen of the sectors affected – so we would suggest, the romance between business and education interests has progressed in a similar fashion. We are advocating a mixed response: one where there is a celebration of mutuality, but also one where warnings are registered about possible asymmetries in the values, interests, and influence that could disadvantage both sectors and spoil, what might otherwise become, a beautiful and reciprocal co-existence.

Roots of Mutual Affections

The role of public education continues to be a prevalent issue in Canadian education. In the past fifty years, Canada has attempted to quantitatively and qualitatively increase the level of education attained by its citizenry in attempt to spur economic growth and social development. Parallel to these developments there has been an increase in social scrutiny over the rising costs of education and the projected rate of return to this enormous financial investment.

In the mid 1900s, Canada began to experience a rapid development of urbanized centres coupled with an increased demand for technically skilled labor to fuel its growing industrialized economy. As a result, society began to place an increased value on education, not only to provide skilled labor, but also develop a well-rounded society. The social benefits attributed to education include increased literacy, responsible participation in society and politics, identification of national goals, improvement in mental and physical health, and development of attitudes and values favorable to progress (Machlup, 1975). In addition, education has long been thought to be a primary generator of economic growth and so, "human resource development [through education] became an important element in economic planning beginning in the 1960s" (Parnes, 1984, p. 22).

The increased demands placed on education can be directly attributed to the parallel increases in the economy and national income. Machlup (1975) states, "as national income increases, the demand for education increases in most countries by a larger percent" (p. 63). He further notes that this relationship is not one dimensional because as income increases, people demand not only more education, but also a better quality of education. Lee (1983) makes reference to the general assumption that an expanded education system would generate a modern, complex and industrialized nation, and most importantly, spur economic growth. The term human capital emerged as a descriptor to the value and importance of people on the economic development of a nation. Cheal (1963) states, "the progress and development of a country is dependent upon its human resources, their members and their qualities, their requirements and their ambitions" (p. 2). To demonstrate the impact of education on economic growth, Lee (1983) replicated and expanded on Peaslee's Optimum Educational Mix Model for economic growth. He found that a strong relationship existed between gross age-specific enrolment ratios and subsequent economic growth.

Education in Canada is considered a prime generator of economic growth for several reasons. Perhaps its greatest effect is to increase productivity by up-grading the skills of the labor force which, in turn, allows for higher levels of efficiency and adaptability to technological change. In addition, Webb, McCarthy, and Thomas (1988) identify enhancement of managerial talents, increased receptivity to new ideas and knowledge, greater efficiency, and improved performance as educational benefits. As a result, Canadian society has placed a high value on education and a well-founded expectation that the rate of return on investments in education will positively influence economic growth.

The business community has tremendous incentive for investing in the improvement of education, though individual businesses might not see the direct and immediate advantage because the benefits are generally distributed. Both business and education experts know that business' acumen in areas of choice, markets, utilization of research and development, and personnel management has much to contribute to the enhancement of public schools. Arrangements between business and education to improve education are seen a mutually beneficial, as well as philanthropic, by businesses. Whether out of social concern, relative to specific problems encountered in education (such as high risk students), or from a sense of social responsibility for the economic development of the local and wider economy, businesses contribute to education with the hopes of gaining future benefits.

In recent years school budgets have decreased in real dollar revenues, and school administrators have felt strapped for resources. According to Glass' (1992) study of the American school superintendency, the most difficult problems facing board members and superintendents related to financial issues as political support and community priorities for the welfare of children were viewed to be on the decline (pp. 43-46). For example, in relation in their job effectiveness in 1992, 59% identified financing problems as their number one continuing problem. Furthermore, 12 percent cited moving to a "better financed" school jurisdiction as their reason for leaving their previous place of employment (p. 47) and 68.7% indicated that the issue most likely to cause them to leave, if not corrected, would relate to financial matters (p. 50). These statements exemplify how policies made in tough economic times may be different from those made during more affluent times. We contend that social and economic conditions should not automatically provide jurisdiction for what would otherwise be considered ethically unjustifiable policies or practices. Unfortunately, these conditions tend to make business-education proposals worth considering in the eyes of desperate school boards, and therefore, heighten the need for ethical awareness and economically hard times.

Varieties of Dating and Match-making Activities

Some of the relations between business and education are unilateral in the sense that a business will make a straight donation of equipment or be involved in cash-sponsoring an educational initiative. Often these are "no strings attached" arrangements that allow companies to raise their corporate citizen quotients by tangible demonstrations of social concern. These are advertised as altruistic and beneficent initiatives. In other cases, coalitions are forged with schools. It is common for existing business coalitions such as chambers of commerce or round tables to work in partnership with schools or school systems. Such coalitions have the advantage of giving individual companies the opportunity to benefit themselves and the schools through their contributions, but avoid direct transorganizational intersections and disperse the risk that might come to one company of the coalition. In other cases, schools are targeted as high prospect markets, with captive markets or future consumers. The exploitation of schools as marketplaces has many considerations impinging on its legitimacy.

Harty (1990) stated that "school children are for sale to the highest bidder" in a fashion even more threatening than 12 years earlier, when she published her report entitled *Hucksters in the Classroom: A Review of Industry Proganda in Schools* (1979). She contended that "market advertising to children is reprehensible because it masquerades as education" and makes knowledge a means to an end. Harty pulls no punches and assumes no generosity in her assessment that "corporate handouts are not simple gifts but sophisticated marketing tools for high-stakes power game that alters power games that alters the purpose of public education" (p.7). She asks "Do we really want the Jolly Green Giant teaching nutrition, Ready Kilowatt teaching energy, and chemical companies teaching about the environment" (p. 8)?

Scrutiny of Courtships: Some Cases-in-Question

Varying degree and directions of concern about the business and education compacts have been expressed by social commentators and educational policy makers (Farrell, 1991; Molnar, 1990, for example). Some educational institutions have entered into arrangements with commercial interests, while others have not. Some leaders, of course, have clearly defined and long established professional and organizational boundaries that determine what kinds of relationships are permissible and profitable. But, some "blushing" and backing off may be detected on the part of other educational policy makers. They seem to be uncertain about how to deal with the complex forces and affections surfacing in response to advances from a member of the "opposite sector." While they may be inclined to pursue the possibilities of a relationship, they are wary about just how fast to move and how extensive intra-sector relations should be.

For example, the contract between the Toronto Board of Education and Pepsi Cola Ltd., gave Pepsi Cola Ltd. a monopoly over the rights to distribute their product in all the board's schools. For $1.4 million over a three year period, the board made Pepsi the sole pop and juice vendor in the system and distributed Pepsi-sponsored videos and student-of-the-month awards. This arrangement brings to the forefront the need for governance in establishing business-education relationships. The Toronto Board of Education was criticized for having lost the focus of its educational goals by viewing students as marketable qualities.

The Pepsi Cola Company response to this depiction in a letter to a national magazine that had carried the story, with a scathing editorial, saying that "An initiative like this demonstrates the fruitfulness of enterprising, innovative partnerships between the public and private sectors. Regarding Canadian education, we are proud to be part of the solution." They claimed to their critics that an independent survey showed 90% of Metro Toronto students favored the arrangement and they had simply won the contract over seven other competitors in a bidding way. In addition to characterizing the deal as a contract with the devil, a devil that makes your teeth rot, one critic presented in the following limerick:

There once was a school board in Trana.

That I thought it had picked up some manna.

Its fortune is rued.

When carping ensued.

A peach became a banana. (Wilson, 1994, p. A2)

Several years ago, The Real Canadian Superstore (Westfair Foods in Canada) offered "Apples for Classrooms" in exchange for cash register receipts. This large retail grocery chain offered to donate a microcomputer to each school that raised $150 000 in sales receipts. The offer was enthusiastically taken up by many school jurisdictions (Chandler, 1992). The non-participating school boards perceived that the Superstore was mainly interested in promoting their corporate image and having students encourage people to shop exclusively at their grocery chain. The offer of computers for schools was conditional on a certain level of sales, with no computer offered if that level was not reached. They were concerned that the retailer's self-promotion was centrally incorporated in the advertising. They saw no direct nor additional educational benefit from their participation in the program. A final concern was expressed that there was a large discrepancy between the price of a microcomputer (about $3 000) and the $150 000 worth of cash register sales receipts. The actual contribution by the company was assessed to be too small to merit entering into relationship. Several rural school divisions are concerned with the economics of their geographic areas; they expressed sentiments of fidelity toward local merchants who had supported their schools in various ways over the years.

Advocates of image, issue, and product advertising agreements have argued that such relations should be increased. One such supporter, Farrell (1991), said "people in industry know what practical and academic skills will be needed for the current and future occupations. This knowledge blended with the know-how of educators about effective methods of instruction can result in a provincial curriculum that is effective, efficient, and relevant to the needs of tommorrow's workforce (p. 3). He added that Canada had become a technology trading nation, whereby, education must provide our youth with the necessary skills to maintain its future development. He advocated new and better models of education, to ensure Canada continues to make a smooth transition into the information age.

Ethical Assessments of Business-Education Relations

How does one know if a particular proposal is "right, good, proper or virtuous?" How should these arrangements be assessed? For many school boards the various configurations of the business and educational relations are at an early stage of courtship: Each party wonders what onlookers will think, what their potential partner's actual interests and intentions are, and what limits and legitimacy of the their intersection might be. We have provided several examples of responses to these questions in earlier sections.

In attempt to gain a greater understanding of the scope of business-education relationships, we contacted the superintendents of the 25 largest school boards across Canada. We asked them to supply us with any documents or policies they had developed that would define their relationships with business interests. The responses garnered indicated that most school boards do not have specific policies in place to cover business-education relationships. School District 15 of Bathurst, New Brunswick typified the responses by stating, "while actively involved in a number of community/business partnerships, we do not have an explicit policy that deals with this area." However, the Edmonton Public Schools of Alberta and the Delta School District of British Columbia did respond with district policy and procedure statements.

The Delta School District procedure on business-education relationships begins by stating, "It is the responsibility of the principal of a school to ensure that school premises shall not be used to display, distribute, or otherwise advertise a product service or function on behalf of any person, business, or organization unless the principal is satisfied that . . ." The procedure goes on to describe the specific types of desired relationships actively sought by the school district. Edmonton Public Schools also suggests that "partnerships should be mutually beneficial to both the school and the business and should focus on human rather than financial resources."

In sum, our preliminary funding indicate that business-education relationships are prevalent and that few school boards have policies in place that cover such partnerships. The expectations provided by the Edmonton Public Schools and the Delta School District are exemplary of what is needed to establish mutually beneficial relationships in the future. What is left unsaid is what warrants and under grids these policies. This is the role of ethical analysis.

Our hunch is that the absence of explicit ethical analysis normalizes unnecessary confusion in school systems; but that consideration of ethical questions will displace this confusion with a reasonable confidence. We would claim that is ethical criteria, whether institutionalized in policy or consciously and explicitly applied in each case decision, would help both sectors immensely. When special inter-interests arrangements are established, experienced, and studied, then ethical learning, growth, and well-founded comfort results (Kolb, 1990; Schon, 1983, 1987).

The last few decades have seen increased societal concern about the level of ethical behavior shown by corporations, and, in some instances, by educators (Hunter, 1990; Lewis, 1990; Natale, 1990). Ethical questions are an essential part of all human organizations because the goals of the organizations are determined by human values (Hodgkinson, 1991). Ethics should be understood to be the discipline that concerns itself with overall normative constraints and motivations of policy processes and are typically assumed to be grounded in the ambition to be ethically wise and virtuous, and consistent with obligations. We advocate the use of the so-called "Arthur Andersen Model of Ethical Decision Making" because much of the North American business world has received the model in their training and education programs. While we acknowledge this adapted decision template is somewhat simplistic, it does help examine important ethical considerations with the following phases:

1. identification and description of basic decision information, assessment of stakeholder values, intentions, and interests, together with determination and delimitation of ethical and non-ethical issues;

2. reaffirmation of criteria for ethical decision making;

3. generation and elaboration of alternate scenarios, projection of ethical implications, and adjustment to practical constraints; and

4. ethical evaluation and reflection on appropriateness of solutions and action.

Acknowledgment of both rational and intuitive biases is an important function of the decision processes undertaken by both business and educational parties. These biases provide a starting place for what Strike (1993) calls dialogical competence: "the ability to talk about, reason about, and experience appropriate phenomena via a certain set of concepts" (p. 105). Strike says that moral principles, and background conceptions or convictions are important (pp. 107-108). We concur, believing that issues will be more readily addressed, and proposals for relations best considered, if predetermined principles, precepts, and precedents serve as plumb line-type criteria for policy decisions. For example, strains of utilitarianism offer that the end of action is to be general happiness and affirm those acts, dispositions, and institutions which maximize the happiness of all who are affected by them. The basic question one might ask in determining the moral status of a business-education relationship could be: "Will this action produce greater overall well-being for the stakeholders in our school jurisdiction, or the shareholders in our company?" For some utilitarians, well-being is the only good, and they consider their own well-being as neither more or less important than the well-being of anyone else. If one were to retain utilitarian principles such as these to determine the moral worth of a business-education relation agreement, the benefits and costs of either acceptance or rejection would need to be projected. A quantitative approach to this analysis might include such factors as are included in Bentham's calculus (1948, pp. 30-31): intensity, duration, certainty, and propinquity to estimate the benefit produced by any act, practice, or decision. He also identified fecund (chance that more of the same good benefits would follow), purity (chance that the opposite of good benefits would not follow), and extent (the number of people affected by the act). The foci for this variety of utilitarian decision making is the short and long term impact on others, together with the net welfare for key stakeholders.

Alternatively, the theories of rights (Hobbes, 1958; Kant, 1964; Locke, 1952) and deontological ethics provide for criteria-based decisions based on moral entitlements and obligations. Moral obligation theories consider factors other than (or as well as) the ends of action to determine their rightness or wrongness. From a deontological position, a policy is right when it conforms to a relevant principle of duty. Obligations may be either self-imposed, socially-imposed, or divinely imposed (Holmes, 1984, p. 69). A policy decision is deemed appropriate if it respects the rights of all individuals affected by the policy. In short, the security of sustained respect for persons and the impartial nature of a policy will take precedence in decision making about business-education compacts.

Various theories of justice (Rawls, 1971; Walton, 1991) may also offer to help to resolve conflicts of rights and interests with respect to business and education relations. One way of dealing with justice is to give each constituent group its due, according to its work and its predisposition to dependence. Justice focuses on fair processes and an equitable distribution of the benefits and burdens imposed by a policy. Both education and business sectors might easily apply such theories to potential relations and their judicious regard for negative and positive distribution of goods.

Ethical theories have the promise of helping educational policy makers deal with the cases that come before them by generating principles or, in some instances, tie-breaking criteria where conflicts of interests seem to exist. These principles may be expressed in the form of statements or questions that are useful for determining consequences, rights, obligations, and best remedies for stakeholders. Whatever framework for ethical analysis is used, it should admit of and adjust to the practical and social realities of school systems and communities.

School administrators indicate that teachers, students, and parents rely on educational leaders to protect them from counter productive influences and commercial predators. Observers will note that from book covers to lunch boxes, from coloring books to comics, from T-shirts to hats, from radios to toys, everything in the child's world seems to have become ad space. While the alternatives might include monitoring the space, stifling commercial exploitation, or exploiting the phenomenon, school boards, administrators, and other stakeholders need to consider carefully where they want their policies to lead and what, if any, ethical constraints they wish to impose on their own participation in relations with other sectors.

Conclusions

Business involvement with schools has obviously raised some ethical issues. Schools like to think of themselves as untainted by the profit motive (Rist, 1989). However, donations of money of business can be traced back to corporate profits. Furthermore, educational institutions have a "tradition" of commercial involvement with such things as fund-raising, yearbooks, school jackets, team uniforms, and score clocks. Even if only through enlightened self-interest, most CEO's today espouse philanthropy (Carroll, 1989), the ethics of school systems are not necessarily better developed than those of corporations. To reiterate, the value systems, intentions and interests are distinctly different. Although some business leaders argue that their main aim is not to maximize profits (Hunter, 1990), most agree that self-interest is the basis of corporate philanthropy (Sturdivant and Vernon-Wortzel, 1990). The challenge remains for educators to sort through what are the exclusive and common interests of the commercial and educational worlds. Numerous individual and systems forces constrain "good, right, and proper" policy decisions.

In our society, the circumstances indicate a need for business and education to develop closer partnerships (Farrell, 1991; Hoyt, 1991; MacDowell, 1989; Molnar, 1989). Schools require more sources, new ideas, and different approaches. Schools need relations with business to prepare students adequately for our changing society and to gain access to technology. Business benefit in obvious ways from employable and trainable graduates. Business interests enhance their public images by involvement in the educational world (MacDowell, 1989). But details of business and educational partnerships must be carefully worked out. The values of each side must be understood and respected by the other. These differences are not necessarily mutually exclusive but they do exist.

We think that the constraints and permissions of ethically-driven deliberations ought to be the hinges upon which these relations hang. However, the processes by which organization make relationship decisions are not always clear. Sometimes these processes do not consciously or explicitly include the ethical reflection. At times, school system rationales are simply vague. Usually, the welfare of students is the primary criterion for educational decision making; but decision makers must be able to distinguish right from wrong, and not merely in terms of proportional benefit.

This chapter has sought to provide a "broad-brush" description of the relations between business and education. Hopefully this paper will stimulate debate, raise issues for discussion or particularly policy considerations involving the relationship between educational and business interests, and ultimately benefit the inevitability of business-education relations in the future.

References

Alberta Teachers' Association (Nov/Dec 1984). The school/business relationnship: Two views on how close it should be. *The ATA Magazine,* 2-7.

Ashmore, R. (1987). *Building a moral system.* Englewood Cliffs: Prentice-Hall.

Arthur Andersen and Company (1992). *Business ethics program.* Chicago, IL: Author.

Bakalis, M. (1987). Educational business: Words of caution. *Curriculum Review,* March/April, 48-50.

Bentham, J. 1789 (1948). *An introduction to the principles of morals and legislation.* New York, NY: Hafner.

Berg, I. (1971) *Education and jobs: The great training robbery* .Boston, MA: Beacon Press.

Calabrese, R.L. (1990). "The school as an ethical and democratic community." *NASSP Bulletin, 74,* 10-15.

Carroll, A.B. (1989). *Business and society: Ethics and stakeholder management.* Cincinnati, OH: Southwestern.

Chandler, M. (1992). "Superstore computer offer has schools scrambling," *Education Leader, 5(6),* 4.

Cheal, J. (1963). *Investment in Canadian youth.* Toronto, ON: MacMillan Company.

Dunn, M.R. (1987). The effects of corporization on academic medical centres. Paper presented at the Annual Meeting of the American Educational Research Association, Washington, DC.

Farrell, J.H. (1991). "Education-industry partnerships are essential for the 90s," *The Canada School Executive, 11,* 3-8.

Glass, T. (1992). *The study of the American school superintendency: '92 America's education leaders in a time of reform.* Arlington, VA: American Association of School Administrators.

Hobbes, T. 1651 (1958). *The Leviathan.* New York, NY: Hafner.

Holmes, A. (1984). *Ethics: Approaching moral decisions.* Downers Grove, IL: Intervarsity Press.

Harty, S. (1989-90, Dec/Jan). "U.S. corporations: Still pitching after all these years." *Educational Leadership. 47(4),* 77-78.

Harty, S. (1979). *Hucksters in the classroom: A review of industry propaganda in schools.* Washington, DC: Center for Study of Responsive Law.

Kant, I. 1797 (1964). *The metaphysical elements of justice.* New York, NY: Library of Liberal Arts.

Kay, B.W. (1994). An inter-provincial comparison of educational inputs and outputs in Canada. Unpublished Masters Thesis, University of New Brunswick, NB.

Kolb, D. (1990). *U.S. Postmodern sophistications: Philosophy, architecture, and tradition.* Chicago, IL: University of Chicago.

Hodgkinson, C. (1991). *Educational leadership; The moral art.* Albany, NY: State University of New York Press.

Hoyt, K. (1991). "Educational reform and relationships between the private sector and education: A call for integration," *Phi Delta Kappan, 72,* 450-453.

Hunter, J. (1990). "Business ethics: Who cares?" *Bulletin of the Association for Business Communication, 53(3),* 4-6.

Lawton, S. (1987). *The price of quality: The public financing of elementary and secondary education in Canada.* Toronto, ON: Canadian Education Association.

Lee F.P. (1983). School enrolment ratios as indicators of national economic growth. Unpublished Masters Thesis, Concordia University, Montreal, QC.

Lewis, P.V. (1990). "Ethical Orientation for Understanding Business Ethics," *Journal of Business Communications, 27(3),* 213-232.

Locke, J. 1690 (1952). *The second treatise of government.* New York, NY: Liberal Arts Press.

MacDowell, M.A. (1989). "Partnerships: Getting a return on the investment," *Educational Leadership, 47(2),* 8-11.

Machlup, F. (1975). *Education and economic growth.* New York, NY: New York University Press.

Molnar, A. (1989). "Business involvement in schools: Separating wheat from chaff," *Educational Leadership, 47(4),* 68-69.

Natale, J. (1990). "School board ethics: On thin ice?" *The Amnerican School Board Journal 177(10),* 16-19.

Parnes, H.S. (1984). *People power.* California: Sage Publications.

Rawls, J. (1971). *A theory of justice.* Cambridge, MA: The Belknap Press.

Rist, M.C. (1989). "Mass marketers are cashing in on students," *The American School Board Journal 176(9),* 20-25.

Schon, D. (1983). *The reflective practitioner.* New York, NY: Basic Books.

Schon, D. (1987). *Educating the reflective practitioner.* New York, NY: Basic Books.

Strike, K. (1993). Teaching ethical reasoning using cases. In K. Strike & P. Ternasky (Eds.), Ethics for professionals in educatiion: Perspectives for preparation and practice. New York, NY: Teachers College Press. pp. 102-116.

Sturdivant, F.D. & Vernon-Wortzel, H. (1990). *Business and society: A managerial approach (4th ed.).* Boston, MA: Irwin.

Timpane, M. (1988). Afterword. In M. Levine & R. Trachtman (Eds.). *American business and the public school: Case studies of corporate involvement* (pp. 228-230). New York, NY: Teachers College Press.

Walton, C. (1991). *Corporate encounters.* Forth Worth, TX: Dryden.

Webb, D.L., McCarthy, M., & Thomas, S.B. (1988). *Financing elementary education.* Ohio: Merrill Publishing Company.

Weisman, J. (1991). "The new player: Educators watch with a wary eye as business gains clout," *Teacher Magazine*, October, 10-11.

Westrum, R. (1991). *Technologies and society: The shaping of people and things.* California: Wadsworth.

Wilson, L. (1994). "Pepsi's deal with school board raises questions." *The Star Phoenix.* Saskatoon, SK, March 14, A2.

Wright, L. (1989). "Business and education: A symbiotic match," *Principal, 69(1).* 18-19.

Young, B. (1986). "The intervention of business corporations in education," *Canadian School Executive,* September. 14-16.

10

Program Delivery: What New Technology Promises

Arnold Novak

Education systems in Canada today are at a critical crossroad. At a time when society and economic survival depend increasingly on a highly educated population, we are actually experiencing a deterioration of quality of education due to severe budget cuts and general lack of support for school systems (Worzel, 1996). Recent research in both Canada and the United States has consistently indicated a universal problem in that expectations for educational achievement are not being met (Wilkerson, 1994). In 1987, Radwanski reported that at a time when we should be focused on a highly educated population, approximately one out of three young people in Ontario were dropping out of high school before completing grade 12. Furthermore, according to Radwanski (1987), our educational systems are producing "psychological drop-outs" who settle for minimum requirements for a diploma, then enter adult life still deficient in the knowledge, skills, and attitudes needed to function effectively in today's complex and demanding society.

Society is changing rapidly in terms of skills required to compete and even exist in the information-driven age of the next century. According to Hathaway (1990), our education systems still use the organizing principles of mass production and are still modelled after the Industrial Revolution of 150 years ago, yet there won't be any mass production-type jobs when our students graduate. Education systems for the twenty-first century need to undergo mass customization, which would involve developing a unique education curriculum, a unique set of educational tools, and a unique set of educators for each and every student (Worzel, 1996). Our school systems and curriculum should be focusing on how to develop self-directed learners with skills to engage in critical thinking and problem-solving (Roblyer et al, 1997). In order to educate for a world-wide economy and develop entrepreneurs for the twenty-first century, education system must deliver instruction that is not reliant upon time, space, culture, age, and diverse value systems (Wilkinson & Sherman, 1991). Are our educational systems ready for this and if they are, do they know how to get there? Technology seems to hold the promise of solutions to some of the current educational problems and this chapter will examine what technology really involves and how it might provide some important solutions to the problems of educational program delivery.

What is Technology?

The word "technology" and its association with innovation and change has a long history. In his book "The third Wave," Alvin Toeffler (1980) used the analogy of a rearview mirror to analyze the development and role of technology. He describes our recent history as falling into four periods; the Nomadic Period (pre-8000 BC), the Agrarian Period (8000 BC to 1700 AD), the Industrial Period (1700 AD to 1955 AD), and the Post Industrial (Information) Period (post-1955) (Hathway, 1990). An examination of these periods in more detail reveals three interesting features: first, the transition from one period to the next was precipitated by significant advances in technology, such as machines running factories and then computerized systems running the machines which run the factories. Second, technology, in whatever form it takes, provides new and better tools and changes the nature of work and the way people do the work. Third, technological advances bring about an accelerated rate of change, a rate which people must recognize and work with. As we look through the rear-view mirror, it is important to recognize that each technological advance has changed the way work was done, and the way education was organized and provided. (Hathway, 1990).

When most of us think of technology, we think of hardware items such as the television set, the computer, or the communications satellite. Technology, according to Heinich and Molenda (1995) is neither the hardware nor the software, rather it is putting knowledge to work to solve specific problems. That is to say, the true technology lies what we can do with these products, such as network with professionals around the world, access and manage information with our desk-top computer, and design instruction which is specific for a learner situation. Saettler (1990) argues that technology should be looked at as a process rather than a product, focusing on the process of applying the hardware and software for educational purposes. Muffoletto (1994) describes technology not as a collection of machines and devices but rather a way of thinking and acting. According to the Information Technology Association of Canada (1989), the key to technological enhancement is to create empowering environments to enhance the learning process.

Program Delivery

The true value of technology lies in how it can solve educational problems, by enabling educators to deliver a more relevant program which focuses on the needs of the learners. Program delivery in this context will include: accessibility to instruction and information, education within diverse classrooms, adapting to curricular changes, and developing more cost-effective approaches. These issues shall be examined to determine whether some of the technological advances hold any promising solutions. As suggested previously, advances in technology have not only created many of the problems related to change, but have also provided some good solutions.

Accessibility

A successful educational program requires a high level of accessibility for all participants, including learners, teachers, and administrators. Accessibility of instruction involves enabling all learners to access curriculum-based courses or programs either locally or at a distance, and with the flexibility of time, place, and learning format. This includes students who are disabled or handicapped, who are denied courses or programs because of limited resources or distance from the school, or who find themselves in an instructionally-impoverished environment. Teachers require accessibility to varieties of curriculum ideas and materials, current professional ideas, and to have opportunities to communicate with other teachers and feel a part of a community of professionals. Administrators likewise need access to a variety of information dealing with professional research, school policy, and day-to-day operation of the school. In all of these cases, program accessibility can be improved with technological advances in distance education, the information technologies and computer-based instruction.

Few educational practices in recent years have caught more of the attention and interest of educational policy makers as the concept of distance education. According to Barker & Dickson, (1996) this interest has been driven by reductions in educational budgets, teacher shortages in certain subject areas, new curricular demands, and an increased desire to broaden educational opportunities for students, regardless of their geographic location. Typically, distance learning involves a master teacher delivering instruction in synchronous time (real time) or asynchronous time, from one distant site to one or more multiple sites, using a combination of audio and/or video technologies. This is made possible with fully interactive two-way audio and video systems utilizing the transmission technologies of fibre-optics, micro-wave, or satellite. Distance learning is becoming increasingly effective in terms of quality of instruction because teachers and learners can be fully interactive using technologies such as computer-based learning, networked-learning, and direct on-line learning. Innovative instructional approaches such as collaborative learning, self-directed learning, and problem-based learning can also be designed into distance learning courses to maximize the level of student participation and engagement. Distance education holds tremendous promise for equality and accessibility for education because learning is held constant and time and place of learning can vary.

Information technologies such as the Internet and Web browsers are enabling teachers and students to create and participate in virtual learning communities (Sherry, 1996). What makes the classroom of the future unique is that the students can have full access to special classrooms, unlimited resources, and have access to the individual teacher who would be "logged on" or available at that same time. Use of the Web for this level of interactive instruction involves a combination of posting the basic information on webpages, to creating sophisticated virtual classrooms where most of the instruction takes place on-time. Within the virtual classroom, instruction can be targeted toward individual students where special resources can be made available through a "distributed learning" approach. These learning opportunities are independent of time, form, and place, and adapt instruction to individual learning styles by allowing students and teachers to interactively control the delivery of information.

The key to such "networked" learning environments is that they have to be supported by good communication software and provide access to vast electronic databases. These databases go far beyond a typical library or resource centre and allow learners to log on to other computer systems to seek out current information on any topic imaginable and to create a shared knowledge-base. The electronic mail system provides teachers and students opportunities to communicate with each other as well as have access to human resources not previously possible, in both synchronous and asynchronous communication modes. This form of electronic conferencing not only facilitates the communication process but greatly increases accessibility to student questions, comments, reflections, and peer-reviewed reports (Scardamalia and Bereiter, 1994). Increasingly, our students see the Internet and computer technology as a fairly normal part of the learning landscape, reports Roblyer et al. (1997). Indeed, educators must recognize the importance of ready-access to people and resources because "where knowledge is power, communication is freedom" (Miller & Clouse, 1994).

In an attempt to make learning accessible to many types of learners, computer multi-media systems have become very popular. Multi-media programs incorporate sound and images stored in different devices and amalgamated through computer software into an interactive program (Heinrich et al, 1996). Multi-media systems can provide a structured program of learning experiences to individuals and groups, with special emphasis on multi-sensory involvement. Likewise, computer-based interactive video creates a multi-media learning environment which also can be made accessible to different learners, in both a physical and cognitive sense. Significant advances in learning software has changed computer-assisted instruction from merely drill and practice machines to integrated learning systems (ILS). Students work through lessons as prescribed by the built-in management system which not only prescribes the level of content but tracks individual student progress. The strengths of computer-assisted instruction lies in its ability to be adapted to any age of learner and practically any level of cognitive or physical development. The sophisticated level of learner management makes computer-assisted instruction available to many levels of learner as an independent or a cooperative learning system.

Diversity of student population

Perhaps one of the most critical dimensions of today's classroom is that of diversity of school populations. With the general practice of inclusion of special needs learners in Canadian classrooms, educational programs must try harder to accommodate the learning disabled, the physically disabled, the mentally handicapped, and the gifted students. It is here that computer-based learning systems are receiving attention because of flexibility and interactivity of instruction. The network-technology systems allow learners to communicate with each other and maximize their abilities with less frustration and more empowerment to succeed. Adaptive devices such as voice recognition systems can help learners with severe visual and physical handicaps. Multi-media systems can accommodate students with different backgrounds, beliefs, and learning styles, and provide special needs learners with opportunities to learn in a multi-sensory mode including sound, motion, and interactivity. The special needs of these learners is the flexibility of time so they can learn at their own pace, whether this be slow or accelerated rate. Computer-based instruction has good promise in meeting the wide range of individual needs. Whereas a structured, drill and practice approach might be appropriate for some, a more flexible, non-linear program using hypertext technology would be more challenging and engaging. Networked learning and having access to a wide range of resources can greatly assist to integrating minorities into a more cohesive social structure and begin to address the special needs of multi-culturalism. Technological advances in computer software and telecommunications are making great strides in meeting these challenges to connect special needs learners to each other and to appropriate learning resources.

Meeting curriculum needs

Today's students, whether they live in urban or rural schools, are growing up in an age focused on electronics and communications. They are receiving much of their information from television, computers, video games, the internet, and a vast array of other electronic resources. Our school systems for the most part are trying to keep up to this increasing electronic literacy, but there appears to be a perceptible gap between these efforts and changes in local curriculum (Barker and Dickson, 1996). Many would argue that traditional learning modes no longer work and no longer challenge learners. Education must make use of new and advanced tools that are able to bring information from the outside world into the classroom and at the same time transport student learning beyond the walls of the school.

Technology, as a tool for learning, enables teachers to implement the curriculum in different ways. Teachers can improve curriculum by accessing may forms of alternative resources and improve the learning process by promoting active learning through work of complex projects, thinking about and challenging assumptions, and discussing current topics. Technology can support project-based learning by providing a more information-rich and resource-rich environment. Technologically-driven instruction supports collaborative learning because it can provide opportunities for learners to reflect, communicate, and interact in an environment where the pace and time of communication is flexible and meets the needs of the learner. Opportunities which include networked-learning greatly improves the quality of teacher-student interaction and enhances the feedback process (Cates, 1993). However, we are reminded that the key to all of this is curriculum change and that this is typically a very slow process (Willis, 1992). Improving this process ultimately means focusing more on the individual learner and shift away from the perceived needs of society or government.

Cost-effectiveness within program change

Cost effectiveness for program delivery deals with access, productivity, and quality. With our ability to maximize uses of human and learning resources through distributed learning, program accessibility is increasing rapidly. Teachers can become more productive through training in technology-based methods and quick assess to accurate information that can help them meet individual needs. Productivity can be increased by using word processors, spreadsheets, and databases for record-keeping and report-writing, graphics and desk-top publishing for preparing instructional materials, and test-generating programs for student assessment. Technology can increase teacher-efficiency by placing computer-power directly in the hands of teachers so they can achieve betters results by standardized instructional methods and decreasing personnel costs (Reigeluth & Garfinkle, 1992). This idea would support teachers as an integral part of the instructional process and that technology tools will empower them to teach better, to use their time more productively, and impact the efficient system of delivering instruction.

Historically, cost of technology was considered prohibitive for schools and school systems. Distance education, when compared to the traditional classroom instruction, did not produce the same learning results. Recent studies have shown this is no longer the case, as improved course design and networked learning has shown distance learning to be quite an effective approach. In terms of cost of delivery for interactive television, this too is reducing through advances in microwave transmission and computerized on-line learning. In the case of two-way audio, audio conferencing using telephone lines into a connecting "bridge" can accommodate two-way communication with amplified audio at very reasonable cost. Interest in distance education is increasing and being driven by popular interest in the Internet and the World Wide Web where costs are relatively low and accessibility is high.

Technology and the Teacher

For most of us, including teachers, the mention of technology in education immediately brings to mind the use of some sophisticated devise or set of equipment. A decade ago, radio and television were the state of the art technologies, now most educators will defer to technology as the computer (Muffoletto, 1994). Although there have been significant technological advances in communication and mass media because of the development of computer technology, there is little evidence to suggest that technology has impacted education to an extent where it has changed the way educators do their work. Rather, "technology in education has amounted to little more than additions of capital and equipment to an already labor-intensive system, but significant increases to productivity" (Hathaway, 1990).

One of the reasons the impact of computers has been slow is that technology has been perceived as a substitute for what the teacher already does well, namely to teach. To a large degree it has not changed how the work of teaching is done and therefore has not enhanced education. Part of the difficulty in applying technology in education may involve keeping the subjects of instruction separate from the processes of instruction. Technology presents itself as the subject of instruction at the same time it offers information management tools which may alter the teaching process itself. In situations where teachers have not received more than adequate training to be able to use the computer as an integral instructional tool, teachers are placed in unfair competition with technology and are doomed to stress, fear, and failure. It becomes very important to identify the right roles for teachers and the right roles for technology.

Success of an innovation has been determined by how it has been used. History has shown over again that a new idea does not become significant technology until it can be used to solve practical problems. Just as the written text of ancient Greece was to change the face of education, so too was television in the 1970s and the computer in the 1990s. However as we know, motion pictures did not replace books and television did not replace the teacher. It still remains the case that so far computers are still not being strongly embraced, and that's probably due to teachers and administrators still not identifying their full potential. Until we reform our perceptions of learning, technologies will continue to be delivery vehicles and not tools to work with (Jonassen, 1995). Fullan (1987) continues to be a strong proponent of the need to train educators to properly use technology. He states that professional development is critical for the dissemination and implementation of educational innovations, and thus determines its success. Training which focuses on pedagogical and instructional aspects of computer use contribute significantly to computer integration (Roblyer et al., 1997)

Technology and the Learner

An educated person should be a knower, a thinker, and a learner (Jonassen, 1995). This requires very deliberate strategies and different approaches to curriculum development and implementation. This ultimately means the teacher's role must change from an adaptor of curriculum to a designer of instruction. With the increasing capabilities of the internet to transmit text, graphics, audio and video, teaching and learning will become predominantly an on-line process. This process has teacher and learner interacting with each other as they interact with ideas and resources. In order for this to happen, materials must be designed for the individual learner and their learning requirements. The challenge of providing teachers with time, resources and knowledge to generate course materials for use in these new instructional contexts becomes even more critical.

One of the most important skills we can give to students is that of self-learning which is indeed one of the clear benefits of technology. Computer technology has tremendous potential for guiding the learning process because of the capability of managing extensive amounts of information and controlling or managing the completion of routine and repetitive tasks. As well, technology motivates learners by creating more interesting and active learning environments and providing an element of fun. Technology also empowers students to produce, create (like adults), express themselves, become life-long learners.

An area of learning which is generally overlooked by curriculum developers is that of learner management, how curriculum materials enable learners to direct their learning efforts and how to structure and monitor the learning process. Presently, curriculum is developed by "content experts" with very little contact with the learner population. Learner management is not addressed other than in a large group basis when the teacher tries to move all students through the same activities in concert, and usually taking aim at the middle of the road. This has two problems: first, individual differences are not really considered, and low and high achievers remains at risk of not directing their own pace of learning. Second, the education program relies more on the trained teacher to devote the majority of their time to learning management than on the active learning process. This model is quite costly because it requires a low student to teacher ratio in order for the single classroom teacher to remain in control of learning. An important role for technology could be to help structure and monitor the learning process, leaving the teacher more time for facilitating the learning process and guiding learners to new vistas.

Conclusion

Education systems face challenges of outcomes, accessibility, and cost. This chapter has described how new technologies are addressing many of these concerns. As learning outcomes become more specific and defined, technological approaches can assist the learner to reach intended goals through human as well as electronic support. Accessibility to a variety of courses and programs can provide students with a wide variety of study options. Distance learning can accommodate individual learners as well as small and large group configurations and can address learner differences, whether cultural, physical, or psychological. The learning process is improved because learners are more actively engaged and have a greater motivation to be responsible learners as they work within a learning-community environment.

Above all, the purpose of schools should be the education process and the purpose of policy makers and administrators should be to support the process. Technology, it is argued, can help to support the process by making instruction more rich and accessible, and by making more cost effective. In terms of improving learning, once students have full access to the Internet and under the guidance of skilled teachers, students will become information-explorers, navigators who use technology tools to locate, exchange, and analyze digital information. Students will learn to take more responsibility for their own learning and will collaborate with others to find new information outside of the classroom walls. It is expected that the role of teachers and students will periodically change where students become teachers and teachers become students. In all of this, teachers serve as facilitators guides, and co-learners with their students.

Distance learning's future will see the convergence of a mix of technologies to deliver instructional content as well as to promote interaction between students and teachers. Print based materials will continue to be used as a major medium of instructional exchange, but will increasingly be transmitted digitally, as will images, motion, and sound. The real future of technology lies in application of good instructional design whereby the goal of any instruction is learner-focused and designed to overcome a deficiency of skills or knowledge of a learner. Careful determination of the instructional task provides the designer with clear guidelines in terms of content organization, sequencing and pacing and provides the learner with structure and success.

The cost of program delivery should be able to be reduced as resources are used more efficiently and effectively. The development of a cadre of master teachers and instructional designers provide cost-efficient means to develop curriculum and instructional resources. The routine tasks of learner management are handled by para-professionals and a more responsible and self-directed learner. Finally, the educational program itself is enhanced through proper investment of resources. A critical part of this investment is the adoption by teachers and administrators. Historically, schools and school systems have often viewed technology as a one-time investment instead of seeing it as a process of system improvement. Too often a great deal of money is invested in technology because it is the thing to do, without much consideration for staff receptivity. Fear often revolves around innovation and the rapid move to obsolescence associated with rapid change. Technology by its very nature is rapidly changing and requires proper utilization, without fear. In all of this, it will be important for educators to maintain a mind-set which receives the challenge and sees technology as a means with which to understand and take advantage of change.

References

Barker, B. & Dickson, M. (1996). "Distance learning technologies in K-12 schools. Past, present, and future practice," *TechTrends, 41 (6),* 19-22.

Cates, W. (1993). "Instructional technology; The design debate," *The Clearinghouse, 66 (3),* 133-134.

Fullan, M. (1987). "Planning, doing and coping with change," In R. Carlton & E. Ducharme. *School Improvement-Theory and Practice*. Lanham, MD: University Press of America.

Hathaway, W.E. (1990). *Education and technology at the crossroads*. Toronto, ON: Captus Press Inc.

Heinrich, R., Molenda, M., Russell, J., & Smaldino S. (1996). *Instructional media and technologies for learning. 5th Ed.* Englewood Cliffs, NJ: Prentice-Hall.

Information Technology Association of Canada (1989). *The enabling effect.* An ITAC report of using technology for strategic advantage.

Jonassen, D. (1995). "Supporting communities of learners with technology: A vision for integrating technology with learning in schools," *Educational Technology*, July/August 60-63.

Miller, C. & Clouse, R. (1994). "Technology-based distance learning: Present and future directions in business and education," *Journal of Educational Technology Systems, 22 (3)*, 191-204.

Muffoletto, R. (1994). "Technology and restructuring education Constructing a context," *Educational Technology, 34 (2)*, 24-28.

Radwanski, G. (1987). *Ontario study of the relevance of education and the issue of dropouts*. Toronto, ON: Ontario Ministry of Education.

Reigeluth, C. & Garfinkle, R. (1992). "Envisioning a new system of education," *Educational Technology, 22 (11)*, 17-22.

Roblyer, M.D., Edwards, J., & Havriluk, W. (1997). *Integrating educational technology into teaching,*. Upper Saddle River, NJ: Prentice-Hall.

Saettler, P (1990). *The evolution of American educational technology*. Englewood, CO: Libraries Unlimited.

Scardamalia, M. & Bereiter, C. (1994). "Computer support for knowledge-building communities," *The Journal of the Learning Sciences, 3 (3)*, 265-283.

Sherry, L. (1996). "Supporting a networked community of learner," *Tech Trends, 41 (5)*, 28-32.

Toffler, A. (1980). *The Third Wave*. New York: Bantam Book.

Wilkinson, T. & Sherman, T. (1991). "Telecommunications based distance education," *Educational Technology, 12*, 54-57.

Willis, N. (1992). *New technology and its impact on educational building*. Paris: Organization for Economic Co-operation and Development.

Worzel, Richard (1996). *Comes the revolution. teach: Education for today and tommorrow*. Toronto, ON: Quadrant Educational Media Services (p.5).

11

Leading With Less:
Leadership Issues in a Time of Financial Constraint

Patrick M. Renihan and Frederick I. Renihan

In his address to the Royal Society in 1991, Michael Frye reflected upon the current context of organizational life. As many contemporary thinkers have done, he portrayed the reality of a dramatic paradigm shift, on which has triggered change at all levels of society. Spurred by the mentality of transition; encouraged by the impending end of a century and with it the end of the millennium; characterized by a shift from an industrial to an information economy; these changes have drastically altered the ways in which we acquire process and apply knowledge. Such changes present dilemmas that were not dreamed of when this century began. As the line in Max Bygrave's old song goes, "things ain't what they used to be." This applies as much to the educational institution as it does to any other sector of our society. The turnabout may be appreciated more fully if we contrast our current context to that which prevailed thirty years ago:

THEN: Educational choice was a luxury of the few, and was provided on grounds of denomination or wealth.
NOW: Choices are broader and are tied significantly to empowerment and the rights of students and parents.

THEN: Community expectations for schooling were simple and, even tacitly, quite well understood.
NOW: Expectations vary and often place contradictorry demands upon school professionals.

THEN: There was a clear distinction between home responsibilities and school responsibilities. Communities were supportive of school efforts, but left the educational tasks to the educators.
NOW: Communities demand an increasing voice in educational decisions that affect the education of their young people, while the distinctions between teacher roles and parent roles are less clear.

THEN: The technology of teaching was simple, and the choices among alternative approaches were few. Pressures for renewal and upgrading were nonexistent.
NOW: Technology is complex and changing, and it demands a "learning" mindset on thee part of the teacher.

THEN: Populations of students were, or were assumed to be, for the purpose of teaching homogeneous groups.
NOW: There is increasing knowledge of the realities of student variations in ability, behavior, culture and learning styles.
THEN: The flow of financial and human resources to operate the system was predictable.
NOW: Economic uncertainties and a national deficit preoccupation render the task of resourcingg school systems an uncertain occupation.

It has, furthermore, become increasingly evident that the old solutions, the old leadership responses, are no longer appropriate for new realities, and this was some time ago presaged by Albert Einstein who suggested, "the world we have created as a result of the level of thinking at which we created them."

When we talk of leadership, it is in a period of financial constraint in a new, hitherto inexperienced reality. Further, our leadership responses to constraint cannot, it they are to be effective, depend solely upon those responses which have been employed in the past. It is clear that new creative leadership approaches and mindsets are required in order to energize and revitalize a schooling enterprise that has increased, rather than decreased, in its capability to confound.

In this chapter we make an attempt to examine the leadership alternatives and issues which contemporary contexts and financial constraints engender. This is not a simple task, given the comment by Bennis (1959) as he reflected upon the disturbingly blurred and confusing nature of the literature on leadership:

> Of all the hazy and confounding areas in social psychology, leadership theory and undoubtedly calls for nomination. And ironically, more has been written and less known about leadership than any other topic in the behaviourial sciences.

We feel, however, there is a glimmer of hope in some of the recent perspectives on leadership. In the spirit of Einstein's comment we will, in the following pages, provide a synthesis of these perspectives. We will express a preferred view of leadership, one which is based upon reciprocity, the psychological contract which exists among actors in the educational enterprise, a redefinition of followership, and an examination of effective approaches to change. Based upon this preferred view of leadership philosophies and leadership we argue there are leadership philosophies and leadership strategies appropriate to scarcity in a contemporary world. We will identify these. First, however, we will clarify what we mean by the term "leadership."

Leadership: A Definition

Three properties represent a significant part of the leadership phenomenon as we define it. They are:
a. that values, while always an inherent quality of leadership, must today be

given even greater prominence;
b. that leadership is a property to be exercised by many rather than by few; and,
c. that leadership is at its greatest potential when it exists under norms of reciprocity.

These are integral to the form which we consider imperative for leadership in contexts of change, uncertainty, ambiguity and threat. We define leadership, therefore, as involving those activities and processes which people in organizations consistently enact in order to clarify and refine their own values and the values of those with whom they work. This is not an activity in the exclusive domain of those charged with formal authority. It is, rather, the preserve of all those imbued with a fundamental sense of the importance of the work in which they are engaged.

As we have indicated, our definition of leadership also involves the recognition that leadership and followership are not constant processes that remain vested in the same individuals across organizational activities. Leadership is both emergent and transformational, in the sense that it is at its best when it is formally and visibly promoted within the organization, not as delegation but as a broad recognition of leadership capability in the interests of:

member motivation
  empowerment
  detection of destructive forces
  capitalization upon resources
  systemic leader development
  cultures of interdependence
  problem-solving
  environmental scanning

Faces of Leadership and Faces of Followership

It seems that the distinctions between leadership and followership have become increasingly blurred. As the reader might gather from our definition, this is not necessarily a bad thing. The old phrase admonishes. "lead, follow or get out of the way!" We would reframe this as "lead (sometimes), follow (sometimes) and get out of the way (sometimes)" in the best interests of getting the most out of people in circumstances when the expertise and skills are called for.

Organizational behavior texts are replete with accounts of the impacts of predominant, unchanging leadership modes upon their respective "followerships." Faces of "leadership," in short, engender faces of followership that are not always productive. We have seen that a leadership of exploitation engenders a followership of docility; a leadership of authority engenders a followership of blind obedience; a leadership of domination cultivates a followership of dumb compliance; a leadership of regulation and bureaucracy can create a followership of immaturity and pseudostupidity; a leadership of manipulation spawns a followership of gullibility; a leadership framed in the virtues and charisma of one person brings with it a followership of admiration, adulation and ultimately, reliance. These leadership stances, one might argue, have all had their place; but, a climate of constraint and uncertainty calls increasingly for a leadership of reciprocity, which in turn can do nothing else but engender a followership of reciprocity. That is what we need in order to capitalize on what Miles (1965) referred to as the "reservoir of untapped resources" which constitutes our educational organizations. Elaborating upon a very useful discussion by this topic by Smith (1996) we suggest that the following part of leading would include:

>   creating an environment for creativity;
>   asking questions instead of giving answers;
>   providing opportunities for others to lead you;
>   doing real work in support of others;
>   becoming a watchmatcher instead of a central switch;
>   seeking common understanding instead of consensus; and
>   providing an opportunity for talent and expertise to be developed and recognized.

Three Promising Perspectives

In preparing for this chapter, we scanned the recent leadership literature for perspectives which could shed further light on issues of leadership in a climate of constraint. Three emerged as well worth incorporating in this synthesis and discussion, and each has a message worthy of consideration by those who will be at the heart of the educational enterprise as it moves into the 21st century.

Perspective #1: Welcome an "Unheroic" Leadership View

Murphy (1988) notes that the prevailing model of leadership has for many years been one of "the lion on the Savannah," a "heroic" model, in which the leader has been the key source of the organization's blueprint and who, of necessity, possessed the personal vision to direct the organization. Inherent in the model is an expectation that the formal leader be knowledgeable, strong, tenacious, a forceful communicator and the critical problem solver. Murphy makes a strong case for relieving individual leaders of the impossible expectations which have been set for them . . . to take the phenomenon down from the pedestal. This view of leadership would view "unheroic, leadership" as the approach to leadership in times of economic constraint: a view in which shared vision, an awareness of weaknesses, an ignorant searching attitude and a conscious dependency are the critical qualities. We would agree with Murphy. It is time to be more realistic in our expectations of leadership in the interests of risk-taking, helping others define problems and helping people to let go of their individual monopoly on solutions.

Perspective #2: Understand that Different contexts and Cultures Require very different Leadership responses.

An interesting and useful metaphor for leadership in contrasting cultures and circumstances is presented by Mitchell and Tucker (1992), which the distinction is made between "frontier" and "settled" cultures. It stands to reason that leadership responses are drastically different in each. We believe, as do many others, that many leaders cannot adapt very well to such changes and that, as times change, qualities that once distinguished them as effective no longer serve them well. In Figure I, adapted from the work of Mitchell and Tucker, some of these major qualities are contrasted.

Frontier Cultures	Settled Cultures
Restructuring, redirecting to meet new conditions	Part of an established settled system
Life is rough, danger is everywhere	Established norms guide
People band together for support need for shared commitment	Tasks and relationships are well specified
People band together for support need for shared commitment	Tasks and relationships are well specified
Leadership requires culture building and problem solving	Leadership rests on coordination and expertise
Dynamic management and aggressive leadership are required	Supervision/administration are dominant processes

NEED FOR BALANCE

To devote skill and energy to supervising well established programs, managing resources fundamental changes

Figure 1: Contrasting Leadership Demands of Frontier and Settled Cultures (Adapted from Mitchell and Tucker, 1992)

Perspective #3: Knowing When It's Wartime

Bardwick (1996) introduces a powerful and very relevant metaphor when she differentiates between peacetime management on one hand, and wartime leadership on the other. As the terms suggest, the conditions of comfort, stability, predictability, and orderliness characteristic of peacetime are seen as much more conductive to non-emotional management responses. Leadership, however, is emotional and is the response required to order the "wartime" conditions of change, crisis and urgency.

Employing the wartime metaphor, therefore, to contexts of educational organizations in conditions of scarcity and uncertainty (which for a great many educational executives would not be too difficult) the critical roles would seem to be:

>   defining what the business is
>   creating a winning strategy
>   behaving with integrity
>   respecting others
>   taking action

Bardwick identifies an additional role; that is "the mediation of conflict among those who want to lead because they think it is wartime, and those who refuse to become followers because they still think it is peacetime." Given that we have already noted that leaders should also be followers, they should, quite naturally, be able to generate followership when called upon by circumstances to do so. It was said of one (now unknown) would-be leader "he lacks one thing in a natural leader; natural followers." The keys to success in that realm would include confidence, certainty, action, strength, expertise, courage, conviction, and optimism. We shall add a few more as our own discussion commences.

Leading With Less: A Synthesis

What, then, do the foregoing ideas offer as advice to those charged with leadership responsibilities in contemporary educational systems? Pulling the contextual conditions and leadership responses together, we can identify contrasting characteristics occasioned by predictability and certainly on one hand, and economic constraint on the other. We provide a representation of these in Figure 2 by way of synthesis.

Constraint has, as we point out in Figure 2, a strong impact upon organizational contexts and ways of doing things. We have little doubt that increasing uncertainty at the levels we have witnessed in educational systems throughout the world has the potential for breaking up the traditional ways of doing things, disturbing the status quo, reframing relationships, and re-writing the tasks and processes of organizations. The potential for conflict is also heightened, given the clearer demarcation of diverse perspectives from individual to individual and from unit to unit as they seek their share of a diminishing pool of resources. Neither is this view of organization a novel one in the organizational theory literature. In their now classic comparison of organizations operating in conditions of certainty and those working in conditions of uncertainty, Burns and Stalker (1961) discovered that when the environment was stable, the internal organization was a mechanistic one characterized by rules, procedures and a clear hierarchy of authority; the organization was formalized and centralized, with decisions made at the top. In more uncertain environments, the organization was much more organic; looser, flexible, and adaptive. Rules and regulations were less formal, the hierarchy was less clear, and decision-making and communication were decentralized.

IN TIMES OF PLENTY	IN TIMES OF CONSTRAINT
LEADERSHIP CONTEXT	
. Tasks clear and well specified	. Tasks uncertain and changing
. Environment stable and certain	. Environment unpredictable
. Established norms prevail	. New norms intervene
. Conditions of orderliness and comfort exist	. Conditions of crisis and urgency develop
. Status quo predominates	. Change consciousness increases
. Relationships are predictable	. Potential for organizational conflict increases
LEADERSHIP RESPONSES DEMAND:	
. Supervisory, gatekeeping approaches	. Dynamic aggressive approaches
. System management, quality control	. Redirection, restructuring
. Stability	. Passion, emotion
. Coordination	. Problem-solving
. Culture maintenance	. Culture building

Figure 2: Leadership Contexts and Responses: Times of Plenty, Times of Constraint

Thus, rather than a leadership of culture maintenance, gate-keeping, quality control and coordination, circumstances of constraint and uncertainty necessitate a leadership of mediation, problem-solving, restructuring, in a style which is much more dynamic and emotional than that which has been hitherto required.

We are not convinced that the majority of formal organizational leaders in educational systems have the capacity of capability to make such a dramatic switch. More individuals than we may care to imagine continue to operate as though they are still operating in a context of plenty, either because they cannot change or because they refuse to believe their environment has changed so drastically. What is necessitated, therefore, is a heightened attention to change, and examination of leadership alternatives, and a consideration of means by which educational organizations can engage their own built-in process of renewal. Each of these areas of activity represent significant prescriptions for an organization in its anticipation of constraint.

Leading with Less: Some Prescriptions for Making the Switch

Thus far in this discussion we have argued the point that leadership responses from other contexts and other eras are not suitable for current realities. What is required are new structures and new creative approaches to organizational leadership and organizational problem solving. We have given some attention in our discussion to the types of leadership which would seem most appropriate in times of resource crisis. How such leadership responses can best be facilitated also requires serious consideration. Within the context of educational organizations, this has profound implications for professional development, programs of leadership preparation and succession management. It also requires some introspection and self-analysis for those who occupy formal leadership positions throughout the hierarchy.

In the remaining pages of this discussion, we propose five strategies for facilitating effective leadership responses in a time of scarcity. They are: fostering self-knowledge and self-analysis on the part of formal leaders, developing the leadership potential which exists within the organization, nurturing the environment for creativity and enhancing the capacity of policy makers to support change repositioning the language of the organization.

1. Fostering Leadership Skills of Self-Reflection and Self-Understanding. In another discussion (Renihan and Renihan, 1995) we examined a number of leadership archetypes and their varied, yet distinctive contributions to the culture and success of their organizations over time. We discussed the relative merits of the poet, the statesman, the eccentric, the general, the entrepreneur, the aristocrat, the humanist, the Kamikaze, the advocate and the stoic and expanded upon the idea that leadership is not static, that it is dynamic, developmental, and changes according to time and circumstance.

Furthermore, effective leaders understand the alternative faces of leadership and recognize their own strengths, and limitations in relation to them. This is a strong argument in favor of organizational policies, leadership development assessment strategies, and personal dispositions that provide time and opportunity for leader self-analysis, particularly as it relates to one's work context and one's own skill and understanding regarding the priorities of the organization and the leadership responses they require.

2. Repositioning the Language of the Organization

Central to the business of leadership is talk. Through this vehicle, leaders focus the agenda and shape meaning. They can also set the tone, positively or negatively, for the way in which the important work of the organization is viewed by its key players. Weick (1987) has indicated that this (rhetoric) is a vital leadership quality, and we agree that it should not be under-emphasized. On a similar note, Stephanie Pace-Marshall (1977), in her discussion of sustainable learning communities, suggests that we have excelled in the language of schooling. What we now need to master is the language of learning and life. She suggests:

> If our language is prescriptive, our schools cannot be generative. If our language is static, our schools cannot be dynamic. If our language is linear and algorithmic, our school cannot be playful and creative. If our language is controlled, our schools cannot be mutable.

A school cannot come alive and cannot become a sustainable learning community without a living language that creates living patterns of interaction and relationships; the language of nature and the new learning technologies provide such a lexicon. The creation of ecological learning communities is, therefore, inextricably connected to the language of learning itself. (p.183)

3. Developing the Leadership Potential which Exists Throughout the Educational Organization

A central theme in the foregoing discussion is that leadership potential exists at all levels of the organization. The identification of specific vehicles by which leadership can be highlighted, developed and put to effective use would be well worth the effort. A recent award-winning dissertion (Terracin, cited in Somers-Hill, 1997) for example, examined the conditions under which teacher leadership was most likely to germinate. Among the more significant were: opportunity to participate in significant decisions of the school, engagement in collegial learning, and involvement in school improvement efforts.

4. Nurturing an environment for creativity.

New circumstances, change, austerity, ambiguity, and related conditions highlight, as we have noted, a real need for the identification of new perspectives, new ways of doing things. At times like these, the organization's capacity for "intelligence" is at a premium. Consequently, the promotion of creativity is worthy of serious leadership time and leadership energy.

According to Locke and Kirkpatrick (1995) "the leader must formulate a vision that emphasizes the importance of creativity and must communicate this vision continually to all employees." Among the major strategies postulated by those writers for the enhancement of creativity are:

a. The selection of people who are intelligent, knowledgeable, and tenacious and who use creative thinking processes;

b. Continual training to update knowledge and creative thinking skills;

c. The encouragement of frequent and even heated discussion and communication among team members, among teams, and among all employees;

d. The use of organizational structures that are flexible and give high responsibility (in line with ability) at every level;

e. The rewarding of creative achievement but not the punishing of initial failure. (p. 120)

5. Enhancing the capacity of policy-makers to support change.

We were invited about two years ago to facilitate a retreat organized by senior school system officials in Southern Alberta, and were struck by the theme and the agenda which this group had set for itself. It posed the question: Are we in the way of change? It also provided time for reflection on the concept of change, and for deliberation as to the policy makers' role in facilitating positive change. This initiative was an interesting and encouraging one, not merely because of the theme itself, but because of the very fact that it had been put forward by senior educational officials in the first place, an initiative that indicated a significant awareness among these people concerning their leadership responsibility in such an important area.

The stances taken by school system officials are critical. In Figure 3, we provide a conceptualization of these stances, based upon two considerations:

a. how active the policymaker's role is; and,

b. how positive the policymaker's role is, in relation to the specific change in question.

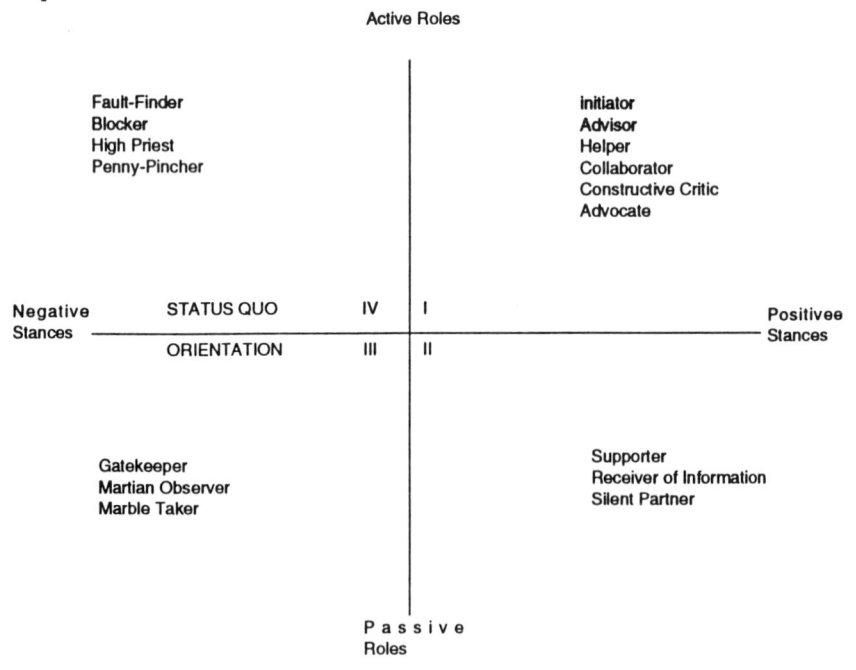

```
                            Active Roles
                                 |
     Fault-Finder                |     Initiator
     Blocker                     |     Advisor
     High Priest                 |     Helper
     Penny-Pincher               |     Collaborator
                                 |     Constructive Critic
                                 |     Advocate

  Negative    STATUS QUO    IV   |  I                        Positive
  Stances  ────────────────────────────────────────────────  Stances
              ORIENTATION   III  |  II

                                 |     Supporter
     Gatekeeper                  |     Receiver of Information
     Martian Observer            |     Silent Partner
     Marble Taker                |
                                 |
                              Passive
                              Roles
```

Quadrants numbered in descending order of constructiveness.

I: Most constructive - IV Least constructive   © P. Renihan
                                                       F. Renihan, 1993

Figure 3: Change Roles and Stances of School System Officials: A Framework for Analysis

This has some value in focusing self-analysis at the policy level, and fostering an examination of motivations behind negative and passive stances (which often serve as sources of aggravation for front-line educators at the school level). How can senior officials support effective change? Much of what we have discussed in the previous pages offers leadership strategies which are critical in this regard. The capacity of senior officials to support change can be enhanced through creative exploration of when and how they might serve as initiators, advisors, helpers, collaborators, constructive critics, advocates, supporters, as mere receivers of information or as silent partners. In any event it demands a greater dialogue among leaders throughout the system than has traditionally been the case in most organizations in past years.

Concluding Comment

Scarcity, as we have noted, presents difficulties which represent a significant part of the challenge facing contemporary educational leaders. Yet they present at the same time some very real opportunities, among which is the opportunity

a. to exemplify creativity and to set it loose, and,

b. to establish some clearer guidelines and patterns for moral standards and moral perceptions as we exercise the leadership role. Hodgkinson (1991), in his discussion of leadership as a "moral art" frames the thought thus:

> . . . these difficulties are the source of peculiar leadership opportunities: the opportunity to discover, clarify and defend the ends of education, to motivate towards those ends; the opportunity to discover means and invent process, since the prevalent state of pedagogic science permits rather than constrains; and the opportunity to create and establish morally grounded evaluation and legitimate it for all the participants in the great cooperative educational project. All of which means that educational leadership is especially difficult, especially challenging and especially moral. (pp.62-63)

In this sense, times of constraint become fairly critical "defining moments" for educational leadership. It is our hope that we have provided some perspective as to the shape which that definition is taking.

References

Bardwick, Judith (1996). "Peacetime management and wartime leadership." In Hesselbein, F.; Goldsmith, M. & Beckhard, R. *The Leader of the Future.* San Francisco, CA: Jossey-Bass

Bennis, W. "Leadership theory and administrative behaviour." *Administrative Science Quarterly.*

Burns, & Staker, B.M. (1961). *The management of innovation.* London: Tavistock.

Frye, M. "Who walked among the stones of fire." Inaugural Address to the 238th Session. *RSA Journal,* 1991 pp. 17-30.

Hodgkinson, C. (1991). *Educational Leadership: The Moral Art.* Albany: State University of New York.

Locke, E.A. and Kirkpatrick, S.A. (1995). "Promoting creativity in organizations," in: Ford, Cameron, Gioia, Dennis. *Creative action in organizations: Ivory tower visions and real world voices.* London: Sage, pp. 115-120.

Miles, Raymond (1965). "Human relations and human resources." *Harvard Business Review,* July-August.

Murphy, J.T. (1988). "The unheroic side of leadership: Notes from the swamp." *Phi Delta Kappan.* May pp. 654-659.

Pace-Marshall, Stephanie (1997). "Creating sustainable learning communities for the twenty-first century." In: Hesselbein, F. Goldsmith, M. & Beckhard, R. *The Organization of the Future.* San Francisco: Jossey-Bass.

Renihan, F. & Renihan, P. (1995). The Changing Face of Leadership. LEADS Annual Policy Conference (unpublished paper). Saskatoon, SK: University of Saskatchewan.

Somers-Hill M. (1997). "Recent dissertations: Creating schools that foster teacher leadership." *Design for Leadership,* National Policy Board for Educational Administration (7:2).

Weick, K. (1987) "The management of eloquence." In: Hampton, D. Summer, C. and Webber, R. *Organization Behaviour and the Practice of Management.* N.Y.: Harper Colins (pp.581-6).